W9-DBC-868

INSIDE

Belize

INSIDE

Belize

Tom Barry

The Inter-Hemispheric Education Resource Center
Albuquerque, New Mexico

Acknowledgments

Without the assistance and encouragement of the Resource Center, *Inside Belize* would not have been possible. Chuck Hosking edited and proofed the book, and John Hawley designed and produced it. I would also like to thank Carla Barnet, O. Nigel Bolland, Grant Jones, Karen Judd, Assad Shoman, and especially Dylan Vernon for commenting on sections of the manuscript. The use of the libraries at SPEAR and the Belize Center for Environmental Studies proved a great assistance. I am especially grateful to the SPEAR staff for making their offices available as a work space while I was in Belize, and I owe special thanks to Carmen Cawich and Dylan Vernon for their help and support. Special thanks also go to the Threshold Foundation and United Church of Christ. As always the administrative assistance of Debra Preusch along with her personal support were crucial.

Table of Contents

Introduction   xiii

Part 1: Government and Politics

Government Structure and Issues   3
    Structure of Government   3
    Nationalist Origins of Modern Politics   8
    The Two-Party System   10
    United Democratic Party   12
    People's United Party   15
    Ideology of Price and the PUP   18
    The PUP in Power: 1989-92   19
Foreign Policy   21
    Belize in the Region   22
    The Dispute with Guatemala   23
    The Two-Treaty Package, 1969-72   25
    Internationalization of Support, 1975-80   25
    Heads of Agreement, 1981   26
    Independent Belize, 1981-90   28
    Independence Recognized and Sea Access Debated, 1991-2   28
    Business Comes First   30
Security Forces   31
Human Rights   33

Part 2: Economy

State of the Economy   39
    Economic Structure   41
    Dependency on Imports and Export Growth   44
    Poverty and Wages   47
    Industry and Infrastructure   48

Sun, Sea, and Ecotourism 50
The Drug Business—Marijuana to Crack 53
The Agricultural Economy 55
Sugar—The Backbone of Export Agriculture 56
Citrus 57
Bananas and Seafood 59
Nontraditional Agroexports 60
Staple Crops 61

Part 3: Society and Ethnicity

A Multi-ethnic, Multilingual Society 67
Mennonites 69
Creoles 70
The Garifuna/Garinagu 73
The Belizean Maya 75
The Ancient Maya 77
Mayan Ruins 80

Part 4: Social Forces and Institutions

Popular Organizing 89
Black Consciousness, Labor Organizing, and Nationalism 89
Cooperativism and Rural Development 91
Politics and Social Justice 92
Labor and Unions 95
A Brief History of Unionism 98
Schools and Education 101
Issues of Higher Education 102
Room for Improvement 104
Communications Media 105
Health and Welfare 109
Church and Religion 113
Nongovernmental Organizations 115
Women and Feminism 119
Immigration and Emigration 123
Leaving for the USA 125

Part 5: The Environment

Conservation and the Environment 129
Mainland Environmental Issues 131
Water Quality and Marine Issues 134
National Parks and Reserves 136

Table of Contents

Attracting the Ecotourist while
    Conserving the Environment   138
The Role of Private Organizations   141
Beyond Conservation   143

Part 6: Foreign Influence

U.S. Foreign Policy   149
U.S. Trade and Investment   151
U.S. Economic Aid   155
U.S. Military Aid   159
Other Foreign Influences   161

Reference Notes

Introduction   165
Part 1: Government and Politics   165
Part 2: Economy   167
Part 3: Society and Ethnicity   169
Part 4: Social Forces and Institutions   170
Part 5: The Environment   172
Part 6: Foreign Influence   173

Selected Bibliography   175

Chronology   177

For More Information   181

Index   183

List of Figures

Figure 1a: Political Districts of Belize   7

Figure 2a: Annual Per Capita GDP Growth   40

Figure 2b: Leading Economic Sectors, 1991   42

Figure 2c: Leading Exports, 1990   43

Figure 2d: Foreign Trade, 1982-1991   45

Figure 2e: Leading Imports, 1991   46

Figure 2f: Export Value of Agricultural Commodities, 1980-1990   56

Figure 3a: Archeological Chronology of the Maya   78

Figure 3b: Areas of Archeological Interest   82

Figure 3b: Areas of Archeological Interest   83

Figure 4a: Education in Belize   103

Figure 4b: State of Health, 1990   110

Figure 5a: Environment in Statistics   130

Figure 5b: Land Tenure and Ownership   132

Figure 5c: Parks and Reserves   137

Figure 5d: National Reserves   139

Figure 6a: U.S. Trade and Investment in Belize, 1990   152

Figure 6b: U.S. Economic Aid to Belize, 1946-1992   157

Figure 6c: U.S. Military Aid to Belize, 1946-1992   159

Figure 6d: Direction of Trade, January-June 1991   162

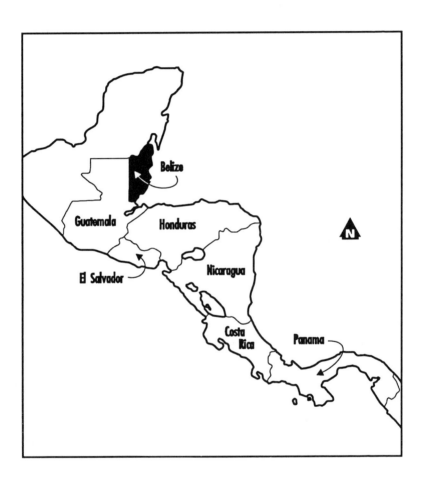

Introduction

Belize, which celebrated its tenth anniversary of independence in September 1991, is a Central American nation that was created out of a backwater British colony called British Honduras. The Río Hondo along the northern border and the Gulf of Honduras gave British Honduras its name, which was changed in 1973 to Belize in anticipation of independence.

The origin of the name Belize is less clear, and like much of its early history, is based on uncertain legend. Mayan scholar Sir Eric Thompson believed the name to be of native origin, coming from *belix* meaning "muddy water."[1] There are also those who feel it is a derivation of *belikin* meaning "land that looks toward the east (or seas)."[2] Others insist the name is a Spanish bastardization of Wallace, the surname of a Scottish pirate who is said to have first harbored inside the reef. From Wallace came the River Wallix which was also called the Río Valís (or Balis) and later became Ballese, and finally the Belize River.[3] An African origin has also been suggested.[4] Pronounced "Bay-leeze," Belize is also the name of the country's chief urban center.

Belize, with its some 235,000 residents (including illegal immigrants), is Central America's least populated nation.[5] But it is not the region's smallest. With its 8,866 square miles (23,657 sq km)—about the same size as New Hampshire—the country is slightly larger than El Salvador and double the size of Jamaica. Unlike most of its Central American neighbors, Belize has not been torn by violent civil conflict and repression. In fact, many Belizeans pride themselves for their peaceful habits unlike the militarized "republics."

Situated south of the Yucatán peninsula facing the western Caribbean, bordered on the north and northwest by Mexico and on the west by Guatemala, Belize is within the northern tropics and has a subtropical climate. Annual rainfall ranges from 55 inches in the

North to 180 in the South, and the average temperature varies from 75 F (24 C) in January to 81 F (27 C) in July.

For a small country, Belize enjoys a diverse topography. The low-lying plains of the North, largely covered with mangrove swamps, are watered by numerous rivers which flow from the low western plateau to the Caribbean sea. The Maya Mountains, rising to 3,699 feet at Victoria Peak, dominate the southern landscape and look over a narrow coastal strip. The Mountain Pine Ridge in the Morth, the origin of the Macal River which plunges 1,000 feet at Hidden Valley Falls, is the pine-covered remnant of the oldest land surface in Central America. Except for the Maya Mountains, limestone and limestone sediments are the dominant geological features in this largely forested and undeveloped country.

A spectacular barrier coral reef lying ten to twenty miles offshore outside the reef and fringing most of the coast protects some 175 cayes (pronounced "kees") or islets dotting the shallow inner coastal water. are the Turneffe Islands, situated 25 miles east of Belize City. At its greatest extent Belize is only 174 miles (280 km) long and 68 miles (109 km) wide.

Belize City is the commercial and population center of the country. At its center is the Swing Bridge, which crosses Haulover Creek. Built after the 1961 hurricane destroyed its predecessor, the bridge is swung aside each evening to allow large boats to head up the river or venture out to sea. The Swing Bridge connects the two halves of Belize City, home of a quarter of the nation's population. A curious mixture of dilapidated wooden shacks, timbered colonial architecture, and newer concrete homes, Belize City is a bustling town built on marshy seaside land—some humorously say on a foundation of broken bottles and mangrove roots.

An increasingly congested urban center, Belize City now commonly has traffic jams and accidents. Motor vehicles, especially taxis, rule the roads in Belize and are not known for either their careful or courteous driving. Traffic accidents are now a leading cause of death in Belize. In 1989 there were 519 casualties (including 35 deaths) from traffic accidents in the country, with a shockingly high number being pedestrians (163) and cyclists (105), and with most of them occurring in Belize City. Increasing crime and drug use, along with persistent urban unemployment in Belize City, figure among the major social problems. For three centuries, Belize City served as the political and economic hub of the colony. But in the wake of Hurricane Hattie it was decided to move the capital inland, and since 1973 the capital has been Belmopan, a civil-servants' town carved out of the Belizean bush some 50 miles to the west of Belize City.

Outside Belize City, which is located in the Belize district, are what city residents call the "districts," sometimes with the clear connotation of the "backwoods." These five outlying administrative divisions have been isolated from national politics and commerce for most of the country's history. In the North are the Corozal and Orange Walk districts, the heart of the sugar industry and the early base of the *mestizo* population. To the west is Cayo, whose urban center is San Ignacio-Santa Elena and which becomes distinctively more Spanish-speaking as it nears the Guatemala border. In the South is Stann Creek, with the Garifuna town of Dangriga serving as its commercial hub. Citrus and banana plantations occupy ever more of its valleys and lowlands. Still farther south is Toledo, the poorest district and the home of the Mopan and Kekchí Maya, its center being the tranquil town of Punta Gorda.

Although Belize still retains much of its frontier ambience, its backwater character is quickly changing as the economy expands, the population grows, and tourism booms. At the start of the 1990s a new airport was inaugurated, two luxury hotels opened, and Belize City finally completed its sewerage system—although the stench of garbage in the drainage canals persists. The national road system is being upgraded and extended. Even Belize City's Swing Bridge, still operated by hand, is due to be replaced in 1992 by a wider one complete with an electric motor.

While the wildlife population has long since been lost in most of the neighboring countries on the isthmus, the dense forests of Belize are still a refuge for jaguar, tapir, crocodiles, and exotic bird species.[6] Regarded as a paradise by some and an uncarved jewel by others, Belize is often subject to devastating hurricanes. In his humorous book, *I Spent It All in Belize*, Emory King (a naturalized Belizean citizen from the United States who decided to stay after a cruise ship he was on crashed into the reef) explains Belize this way:

> Strangers are aghast by the confusion, but we Belizeans are the most tolerant people in the world. The lights go off now and then, the water in the pipes dries up, the phones fail, but so what? No big thing, man. . . . The sun shines, the fish in the sea swim, and the coconuts fall off the trees. We can't starve, and sooner or later all these petty annoyances will go away.[7]

For many, Belize does have all the allure of a tropical island, but life is not paradisiacal for all Belizeans. Large numbers of them in fact leave for the United States to escape high unemployment, dead-end jobs, and empty futures. Health and educational services are inadequate, wages for unskilled work are $10 or less a day, and prices are high since most consumer goods are imported.

A History of Baymen and Slaves

The Spanish were the first to claim the area now known as Belize, having colonized and exploited Mayan communities in the territory during the 16th and 17th centuries.[8] However, it was the British who first settled this territory and other parts of the Caribbean coast of Central America. Pirates from many lands sheltered inside the reef, using small islands or cayes as a base for attacks on Spanish ships. By the late 1600s numerous British adventurers had settled permanently along the coast, making their living cutting logwood used for dye manufacture in Britain. Called Baymen because they lived around the Bay of Honduras, these loggers were a hearty breed who relished their own independence but who came to depend (as early as 1720) on slave labor for the harsh logging work in the Belizean bush.

To assert their claims of sovereignty, the Spanish occasionally attacked British settlements but never seriously mounted a campaign to control the territory. Unable to colonize the area, Spain signed treaties allowing the British to log specified areas of the territory. The Baymen were prohibited from erecting fortifications, governing themselves, and farming. Disputes and small armed confrontations between the British and Spanish were frequent. The showdown came on September 10, 1798, at St. George's Caye when Baymen bolstered by a British schooner chased Spanish ships away from what had come to be known as British Honduras. The nation still celebrates the Battle of St. George's Caye as a National Day. In 1981 Belizeans added another national holiday, Independence Day on September 21.

In the days of the Baymen, work crews of slaves accompanied their owners out to the rugged logging camps in the interior while their families remained in Belize City. The slaves often identified themselves according to which part of Africa they had come from. One section of Belize City was known for many years as Eboe Town owing to the many descendants of the Eboe tribe living there. According to the 1790 census, 75 percent of the territory's residents were slaves, 10 percent were whites, and the rest were either free blacks or free coloreds. Ignored by the census were the Maya Indian communities living in the remote and unsettled reaches of the territory.

Slaves did most of the manual labor in British Honduras, including the construction of St. John's Cathedral, which still stands prominently in Belize City. Most of the slaves and most of the land belonged to a few owners. By the late 19th century, one London-based company, Belize Estate and Produce, owned over a million acres, about one-fifth of the entire country. The concentration of land ownership was also a factor in the colony's dependence on food imports. Even after emancipation in 1838,

British law explicitly prohibited ex-slaves from receiving Crown land grants. This restrictive land policy served to keep labor cheap and available, but the failure to encourage former slaves to become independent farmers contributed to the colony's inability to feed itself.

A Society of Immigrants

Belizean society today is ethnically diverse and culturally rich. Historically it is a country of immigrants, with even most of the Mayan communities tracing their origins to Mexico or Guatemala. The ancestors of the *mestizo* population lived in the Yucatán before the bloody War of the Castes in the mid-1800s forced them to flee. Both groups of black Belizeans—the creoles and the Garifunas—trace their origins to Africa by way of the Caribbean (see Society and Ethnicity). During the 1980s Belize became host of a new set of immigrants as Salvadorans and Guatemalans fled the violence and economic devastation of their homelands.

During most of this century creoles were the largest ethnic group, followed by *mestizos*, Garifunas, and Mayas. But as of the 1991 census, *mestizos* outnumber creoles. This multi-ethnic country is also home to communities of German Mennonites, Chinese, East Indians, and immigrants from the Middle East. Although English dominates, Spanish is spoken throughout Belize. The Garifunas and Maya have their own languages, and an English-based creole is the lingua franca. It is an extremely young population—45 percent of Belizeans have not reached their 15th birthday.

Belize is split almost evenly between rural and urban areas with 52 percent of Belizeans living in one of the 200-plus rural villages. Belize City remains the commercial center but population growth in the other districts is outstripping Belize district, which is 78 percent urban and constitutes about 30 percent of the total population.[9]

Defining the Nation

The main grammar school history book is entitled *Belize: A Nation in the Making.* Since emerging as an independent nation in 1981 Belize has been faced with establishing its own culture and identity. This has proved to be a difficult undertaking. It has meant sorting through the legacy of the British in the country's political, economic, social, and cultural systems to determine what is worth keeping and what should be discarded. Perhaps even more than British influence, the U.S. way of life has penetrated Belizean society—through trading ties and family connections. During the first few years after independence this influence escalated dramatically when U.S. television broadcasts began entering Belizean homes. Watching TV quickly became the favorite national pastime, and this nightly glimpse into the outside world has had the effect of trivializing Belizean affairs and issues.

Defining what it means to be Belizean is not easy, and it can tend to increase social tensions. The debate still continues over whether Belize is a Central American or a Caribbean nation. But even more immediate has been the question of who is the true Belizean—the English or the Spanish speaker, the Belize City resident or the immigrant orange picker in Stann Creek? In a multi-ethnic, multilingual nation, however, there can be no single unifying culture—Belize is a potpourri. There can be a national bird or plant, but not a national food, music, or dress. Rice and beans with stewed chicken is part of the national identity, but so are *tamales* and *garnaches*.

Starting at independence, and particularly since the late 1980s, Belize has enjoyed an outpouring of cultural expression.[10] Much of it rises from ethnic roots, such as Garifuna punta rock music, *fiestas* in *mestizo* villages, and ritual celebrations in Mayan communities. Yet a more national cultural tradition has also developed, seen best in recent literary works. Best known are the novels of Zee Edgell, her latest providing a fictional account of events leading to independence. Belize also boasts of its own short-story writers and poets who are helping to develop a common understanding of what it means to be Belizean.

But this search for a Belizean identity is, in the end, more a collective than an individual undertaking. It involves people in their communities and work places envisioning their future, responding to crises, and acting politically. In facing the future, the Belizean people must determine how much of a Central American nation they really are. They must decide how satisfied they are with a democracy defined by two-party politics and an economy dominated by agroexports and tourism. And they must come to grips with the sensitive issues of emigration, immigration, and racial stereotyping. Belizeans must also come to terms with expanding U.S. cultural and economic ties. In the process of resolving—or evading—such issues, Belizeans will discern what kind of nation they are creating.

Government and Politics

© Tom Barry

Government Structure and Issues

Although it was not until 1981 that Belize was granted independence, the country has a 17-year history of self-government. From 1964 to 1981 the British retained control only over foreign affairs, internal security, and defense. During those years of limited self-government and for the first three years of independence, George Price, the country's first prime minister, and the People's United Party (PUP) were synonymous with government in Belize.

In 1984, after the country's first general elections since independence, Price and the PUP were voted out of office by an electorate demanding a change. The United Democratic Party (UDP) became the ruling party, and Manuel Esquivel replaced Price as prime minister. Despite the economic growth experienced during the Esquivel administration, the PUP, led again by George Price, narrowly won the September 1989 general elections. Winning 15 of the 28 seats in the House of Representatives, the PUP again became the ruling party, although with the smallest margin in the country's political history.[1]

Structure of Government

Government in Belize is guided by the national constitution, which was passed on September 20, 1981, the day before the country gained its independence. Belize, like most of the English-speaking Caribbean, is a constitutional monarchy. Although independent, the country retains a place within the Commonwealth of Nations and a formal allegiance to the Queen of England, who is the titular head of state. Political links between Belmopan and Buckingham Palace are, however, primarily ceremonial.

The constitution provides for a three-way balance of power. The governor general, the prime minister, and the Cabinet—chosen from members of the majority party in the legislature—constitute the executive branch of government. A bicameral National Assembly forms the legislative branch, and there is an independent judiciary. Modeled along the Westminster-Whitehall form of government, the 28-member House of Representatives is elected, while the eight-member Senate is appointed (five by the governor general with the advice of the prime minister, two by the leader of the opposition, and one by the Belize Advisory Council—a constitutionally authorized body of seven members appointed by the governor general for ten-year terms and usually chaired by a Supreme Court justice). Belize has 28 electoral divisions or constituencies based on population and distributed as follows: four each for the districts of Corozal, Orange Walk, and Cayo; two each for the districts of Stann Creek and Toledo; and twelve for Belize district, ten being within Belize City itself.

After consultations with the government and opposition party, the Queen of England appoints a Belizean citizen to be governor general as her representative in Belize. The prime minister is appointed by the governor general and is the leader of the political party that commands a majority of members in the House of Representatives. Cabinet members, who come from either the House of Representatives or the Senate, are selected by the prime minister after conferring with the elected members of his/her political party. These Cabinet members are responsible for the country's ministries. Under the present PUP government there are 11 ministries, with the prime minister holding the portfolio of the Ministry of Finance, Home Affairs & Defense, and Trade & Commerce.[2]

In Belize virtually all bills originate in the executive branch as the product of closed-door Cabinet meetings. Besides reviewing the government's new bills, the House of Representatives is required to approve the national budget. The House of Representatives is equivalent to the House of Commons in England, with the Senate being the counterpart of the House of Lords. After a bill has passed through the House of Representatives it is sent to the Senate for ratification. All new laws require the approval of the National Assembly. Like the House, the Senate can theoretically initiate legislation although not on financial matters. The ruling parties have routinely named as senators party members who were defeated in the general elections, thereby making them eligible to serve in the Cabinet. One critic branded the Senate as a "political anachronism" that is a "house of rejectees."[3]

In Belize the term "government" usually refers to the Cabinet, which includes all the ministers led by the prime minister. The Cabinet ministers are the country's policymakers, operating in secret to discuss and formulate bills and policy.[4] Although individual ministers may disagree in private meetings, they operate under the norm of "collective responsibility," which means they must publicly defend government policy and that each member is responsible for all Cabinet decisions. If a minister is strongly opposed to government policy and feels she/he can no longer submit to the collective responsibility of the Cabinet, that person is expected to resign.

In theory the House of Representatives could serve as a public forum for ruling party members to discuss their differences. In practice, both parties routinely vote as a block. In the highly polarized atmosphere of two-party politics in Belize, party members are disinclined to voice contrary opinions for fear of being seen as "giving ammunition to the enemy." However, the House of Representatives does function as a forum for the political opposition. Since the sessions are broadcast on radio, opposition members can reach a national audience with their views.

The independence of the House of Representatives is undermined by the high proportion of House members who are also Cabinet ministers and by the strict observance of party loyalty. Members of the ruling party who are not ministers are referred to as "backbenchers." Backbenchers rarely exercise any independent legislative role, both because they depend on Cabinet ministers to help satisfy the demands of their constituents and because they normally constitute a small minority. Further ensuring the dominance of the Cabinet has been the practice of both the PUP and UDP governments to caucus all parliamentary members previous to any vote in the House of Representatives. Thus the House is, in practice, a rubber stamp for Cabinet government.[5]

Although the prime minister and his/her Cabinet dominate the system of governance in Belize, effective power rests with the prime minister, who is leader of both the ruling party and the Cabinet. The prime minister presides over Cabinet meetings and sets their agendas. By convention, Cabinet decisions are not the result of votes but are arrived at by consensus—and it is the prime minister who determines the consensus of the Cabinet. The extensive power of the prime minister also includes de facto authority over the country's civil service, with the ability to appoint, discipline, and remove senior public officers, including the heads of police and military. Under the parliamentary system, the powers of the prime minister are counterbalanced by the power of elected members of the ruling party to oust their leader and select another representative. But this has not happened nor is it likely to occur because of the enormous power that the prime minister exercises over the party and government. Although constitutionally a Cabinet government, the government in Belize could better be described as prime ministerial.

A government can fall by a "no confidence" vote in the House of Representatives. This has never happened but might occur if the government has only a thin majority and some members of the ruling party defect or if members of a third party swing a vote to the opposition. General elections must be called by the prime minister within five years. They can be called earlier if the governing party cannot muster enough votes to pass its programs or if the Cabinet chooses an early election strategy.

The judicial branch consists of a Supreme Court and "lower courts" or magistrate's courts. Every district capital has at least one magistrate's court with Belize City having four. Judges are appointed but are expected to be nonpartisan in their decisions and cannot participate in political campaigns. The Supreme Court comprises the chief justice and puisne judges, with appeals from the Supreme Court going to the Court of Appeals. The governor general upon the recommendation of the prime minister and in consultation with the leader of the opposition appoints the justices of the Supreme Court. Minor crimes are reviewed in the magistrate's courts with more serious matters tried by jury before the Supreme Court.

The country is divided into six administrative districts: Belize, Cayo, Corozal, Orange Walk, Stann Creek, and Toledo (Figure 1a). The districts are administered by locally elected, seven-member town boards (with the exception of Belize City which has a nine-member city council). Benque Viejo del Carmen in the Cayo District and San Pedro on San Ambergris Caye also have town boards. Government on the local level is carried out with the assistance of elected village councils that have no independent powers but which assist in the cooperative efforts of the village to promote economic and social progress. In certain areas of the Toledo district the traditional *alcalde* (mayor system) remains in place. Elections to the Belize City Council and the town boards are held every three years. Revenues for the town boards and the Belize City Council are derived from property taxes and trade licenses, supplemented by financing from the national government.

Various statutory corporations and boards round out government in Belize. These include the Central Bank of Belize, Belize Electricity Board, Water and Sewerage Authority, Belize Social Security Board, Reconstruction and Development Corporation, Development Finance Corporation, Belize Airport Authority, National Sports Council, Port Authority, Marketing Board, and Belize Telecommunications Limited (a joint public and private sector company).[6] A nonpartisan Public Service Commission oversees the country's civil service, which is largely unaffected by changes in administration. This absence of a

Figure 1a
Political Districts of Belize

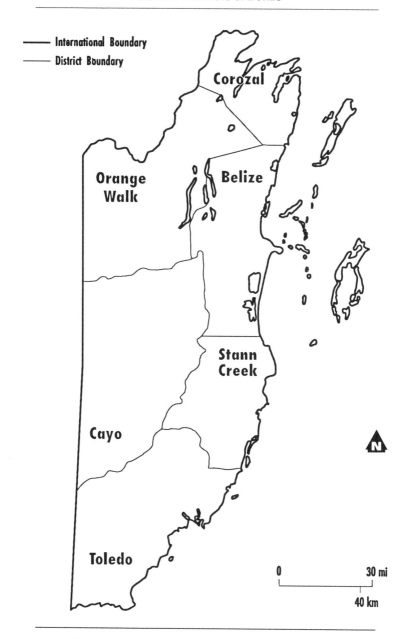

— International Boundary
— District Boundary

Corozal

Orange
Walk

Belize

Stann
Creek

Cayo

N

Toledo

0   30 mi

40 km

spoils system in government is another feature distinguishing government in Belize from that of most of its neighbors.

Nationalist Origins of Modern Politics

Modern Belizean politics sprung initially from efforts to participate in the colonial government, and later to achieve self-government and independence. Economic stagnation in the traditional economic base, chiefly mahogany, and the increased domination of U.S. trade eroded the British colonial hold on Belize in the late 1800s and early 1900s. The emergence of the U.S.-controlled *chicle* (gum base) trade and the predominance of U.S. Catholic teachers in Belizean schools further contributed to the deterioration of the formerly strong economic and cultural links between Britain and British Honduras.[7]

Riots in 1919 by creole soldiers recently returned from World War I constituted the first dramatic sign of rising social discontent in Belize. During the Ex-Servicemen's Riots, Belizean veterans protested the continuing racism in society and their status as second-class citizens. Following these riots a radical nationalist consciousness developed in Belize. In the 1920s and 1930s the Universal Negro Improvement Association inspired by Marcus Garvey gave voice to creole nationalists (see Society and Ethnicity).

Labor organizing, which took hold in the 1930s, also formed an important base for Belizean nationalism and anticolonial politics. Led by Antonio Soberanis, the Laborers and Unemployed Association (LUA), founded in 1937, and later the General Workers Union (GWU), developed a union movement in Belize and laid a popular foundation for the nationalist politics of the 1950s. Besides this working-class base for nationalism, there also existed a critical middle- and upper-class component that sought to expand the political franchise and defend the business interests of native Belizeans.[8]

These elements coalesced into an angry popular rejection in 1949 of a devaluation of the British Honduras dollar. The devaluation was widely seen as benefiting British traders while hurting the poor who depended on U.S. imports for many of their basic needs. The leaders of the ad hoc group that formed the People's Committee to oppose devaluation came mostly from Christian Social Action, a group of alumni from St. John's College formed to promote religious social activism. Two of the most prominent of this group were George Price and Philip Goldson, who soon became the most influential creole politicians in British Honduras. In 1950 the People's Committee became the People's United Party (PUP).

Reaction against devaluation galvanized the nationalist movement in Belize, whose primary goals were universal adult suffrage and self-government. Initially the British and their colonial government regarded the PUP as a radical threat. By the early 1960s they had, however, accepted the inevitability and indeed the desirability of Belizean independence. In 1954 the nationalist movement won its first goal of adult suffrage as well as a new constitution that created a national Legislative Assembly composed of elected members. In 1961 Britain announced that Belize would be granted independence, but it was another two decades before this was done. The long delay was not the result of British stalling but was due to continued uncertainty about Guatemalan claims on the small country. It was not until broad international support emerged for Belizean independence and the British agreed to maintain troops in the ex-colony that Belizeans considered independence feasible.

During the 1960s and 1970s a collaborative relationship developed between the British and the PUP. The PUP guided the country to independence, but not without facing a sizable political opposition. No longer was the PUP the upstart populist party it had been before self-government was granted in 1964. Instead, as the government party it became the target for popular dissatisfaction and discontent. Two principle points of contention for the political opposition were the PUP's campaign for independence and its solution of the Anglo-Guatemalan dispute. The opposition felt that the PUP was handing over too much of the country to Guatemala and that independence would only increase the country's economic and territorial insecurity.

By the late 1950s Britain was ready to dispose of its colonies, but it wished them to retain the current model of government and traditional allegiances. In Belize, as in other British colonies in the Caribbean, Britain felt reasonably certain that upon independence the country would maintain the Westminster-Whitehall model, including such constitutional guarantees as the protection of property and basic human rights, and would retain the British legal system. An independent Belize was also expected to honor its historical trade and foreign policy allegiances.[9]

Despite the anticolonial focus of much early political organizing, there existed wide agreement among all parties that the parliamentary structure of the colonial system was a legitimate model of government. For George Price, "There was no time to waste or to experiment with models. The need was there to organize and the British system was adopted."[10] Thus, early conflict between the colonial government and the nationalists did not stem from the PUP's rejection of the parliamentary system. Rather it was the PUP's early populist tone and its strategy of mobilizing mass popular support to demand self-government that outraged the British. But this tension faded after the PUP accepted the British decolonization plan for self-government. As Assad Shoman explains, "After the British decided that Price could be in the game, he agreed to play by their rules."[11]

More than a decade after independence, Belize remains wedded to a monarchical system while retaining the parliamentary system bequeathed by the British. The overwhelming consensus in Belize is that this system should continue—partly out of a natural conservatism to keep what works, partly from the vestiges of colonialism, and partly due to a realistic concern that switching systems would be taken as a slap in the face by the British. Although the traditional system has provided an appreciable degree of political stability, the failings and weaknesses of the old political structures also obstruct the creation of a more democratic governmental structure in Belize.

The main problem is the lack of effective separation of powers, with the executive and legislative branches joined firmly together by the Cabinet. Because the judiciary is appointed, it does not enjoy the same degree of independence it would if it were directly elected. Another weakness is the rule that Cabinet members must come solely from the National Assembly, limiting the prime minister's choice to men and women who may not be fully qualified to oversee certain ministries. Finally, under parliamentary government the prime minister is not directly elected by all the voting population but only by those from his or her electoral division. Changing these structural weaknesses would have the effect of making Belize a republic—along the lines of Guyana or Trinidad and Tobago, both of which nonetheless remain part of the Commonwealth of Nations.

The Two-Party System

In practice, Belize has had a two-party political system. However, this de facto situation is not constitutionally mandated. Any number of adult Belizeans can present themselves as candidates for the country's 28 electoral divisions. Candidates do not necessarily have to declare themselves to be representatives of a political party. In fact, candidates exist on the paper ballots as individuals not as party nominees, although they are nominees in most cases. Election rules do provide, however, for the marking of different colors opposite the candidates' names indicating their associated parties. The candidate that garners the most votes wins the division seat in the House of Representatives.

Although the two-party system has existed in Belize since 1961, it was not until the 1979 election that the United Democratic Party (UDP) posed a serious challenge to the PUP's hold on government. Both major parties have sought a broad base with supporters from every sector, class, and ethnic group in the country. Combined with the absence of a system of proportional representation (whereby each party would be guaranteed some legislative presence), the well-established dominance and long history of the two-party system inhibit the emergence of a multiparty political culture in Belize. When they do emerge, third parties generally represent the fleeting manifestations of personalities and specific interest groups.

A longstanding concern about the political system is that the country has no laws regulating the formation or activities of political parties. This means that any one person can declare that a political party exists, and the party's victorious candidates are automatically given a constitutional role in government. There also exists some concern about the ability of elected party representatives to switch party affiliations once in the House of Representatives, thereby effectively disenfranchising those who voted for them under their original party affiliation.

Although political parties still sponsor community events to raise money, the parties survive not on membership dues or small donations but rather on major contributions by business donors. There is no system to regulate political finances, yet large donations are still given in secret. Critics suggest reforms both to regulate the registry of political parties and to make all large political contributions public knowledge.

Politics in Belize have always been more a matter of personalities and degree of emphasis than a contest of ideological positions. Both parties seek to avoid class conflicts and to unite all sectors around their often unspecific and ideologically vague platforms. For the most part, affiliation or identification with a political party is not a matter of ideological agreement. Instead political allegiances in Belize frequently follow the traditional political loyalties of one's families and friends or are the result of personal favors (or the possibility of them) distributed by party representatives.

Both parties are proponents of the capitalist system and function in the belief that by representing all classes they help contain class conflict in Belize. When out of office, the parties tend to make more of an effort to identify with the poor majority. During the UDP's term, PUP chairperson Said Musa acknowledged that "there is a tendency, when a party is in government, to take a more conservative stance. History has proven this with the PUP. But certainly while in opposition the party will go on the side of the working class." Musa added that when next in government he hoped the PUP would project "a clear position in favor of the majority of the people, the working-class people."[12]

Having the two parties alternate in office in the 1980s did not clarify the differences between the PUP and the UDP; instead their essential similarity was underscored. Voters saw the UDP resort to the same patron-client relationships for which they had criticized the PUP for many years. The UDP, while more vigorously anticommunist and pro-U.S. than the PUP, demonstrated the political maturity to make many domestic and foreign policy decisions based on practicality rather than ideology. It was the UDP, not the PUP, that extended diplomatic recognition to Nicaragua and the People's Republic of China, while the PUP, immediately upon resuming office, recognized Taiwan and effectively broke relations with China. During the last half of its tenure the UDP government demonstrated increasing awareness of the dangers of a complete liberalization of the economy. The recent PUP administration has shown no sign of radically changing the economic policies promoted by the UDP, but the PUP has promised to place a greater emphasis on redistributing the benefits of economic growth—something that the UDP itself promised to do in its 1989 campaign.

When government is so centralized, national party politics reverberate on the local level. Towns and villages in Belize lack the power and finances either to resolve local problems like sewage disposal and water quality or to manage local resources. Without local political power, the resolution of virtually all issues inevitably involves national government intervention. Therefore, rather than organizing locally to address community problems, Belizeans tend to let matters rest with the party politicians, resulting in a lack of tradition in community democracy and leaving critical local issues perpetually hanging. National government is, however, open to influence from pressure groups and individual lobbies. This open-door policy tends to benefit society's most powerful rather than the weakest. Wealth in Belize is concentrated among the international trade merchants, large landowners, and agroexporters, and through effective direct lobbying these figures generally manage to protect their interests.

United Democratic Party

In 1984 the UDP, under the leadership of Manuel Esquivel, won its first general election with a campaign offering Belizeans a "fresh breath" of politics. Yet the UDP reverted to the opposition in September 1989 after voters returned the PUP to office.

As a party, the UDP has been contesting elections since 1974, and many of its political stars have been dueling in the political arena since the 1950s. It was founded in 1973 as an amalgam of three parties: National Independence Party (NIP), People's Development Movement (PDM), and the Liberal Party (LP). But only the NIP existed as a party in any real sense—the PDM being a 1969 offshoot of the NIP and the Liberal Party nothing more than a small probusiness group that hoped to unite the NIP and PDM under its leadership. The history of the UDP stems from the NIP, which itself represented a 1958 merger of the National Party and the Honduran Independence Party (HIP), an offshoot of the PUP. It was the National Party, a colonial creation to counteract the PUP and the independence movement, which gave the NIP its organized popular base. HIP's Philip Goldson, however, guided this base. The PDM, lead by Dean Lindo, broke ranks with the NIP in 1969, charging that NIP's political focus was too narrow to win an election.[13]

In the 1960s and 1970s the political opposition increased in its appeal to the Belizean electorate. Rallied by the UDP, political outsiders won 38 percent of the vote in 1974, rising to 47 percent in 1979. In this latter election, the opposition stressed domestic economic issues for the first time in addition to its longstanding objection to independence and the PUP's handling of the Anglo-Guatemalan dispute. Campaigning on the slogan "time for a change," the UDP came close to beating the PUP but lost some voter support due to its position against independence and to questions about the competence of party leader Dean Lindo.

By 1984 Manuel Esquivel, UDP party chairperson since 1976, emerged as the party leader, beating out Philip Goldson in a hotly contested party poll in 1983. The UDP presented a stronger, more confident party to the voters in 1984. No longer simply the opposition to the PUP, the UDP offered a conservative platform which stressed the need for foreign investment and private-sector solutions. "We want to see personal initiative and free choice become more a part of the pattern of the lives of individuals," declared the UDP platform.

In preparation for the 1989 elections, the UDP carried out a primary election that badly divided the party between its various political honchos and financial backers. One division arose from an apparent business rivalry between the country's two largest trading houses, with Barry Bowen on one side and Santiago Castillo and Tropical Vision owner Nestor Vásquez on the other. Other factions within the party reflect old divisions based on the three-party foundation of the UDP. Former Prime Minister Esquivel comes from the Liberal Party faction, which had its origins in the Chamber of Commerce, while former Agriculture Minister Dean Lindo, who was ousted as party chairperson in mid-1988 and replaced by Derek Aikman, had led the PDM. Another powerful figure in the UDP is Dean Barrow, who served as foreign minister.

When Prime Minister Esquivel called for a snap election in September 1989, many observers felt that he was a shoo-in based on the country's positive economic performance and the lack of new leader-

ship in the PUP. The government's increased distribution of tax revenues through highly visible development and road-construction projects were also thought to have favored its reelection. But the old
campaigner George Price was ready with a strong platform and a couple of hot issues, notably popular chagrin at the UDP's selling of passports as a source of government revenue.[14] Although it did retain 13
seats in the House of Representatives (reduced to 12 after one representative later switched to the PUP), the UDP once again assumed its
old role as the opposition party.

In a post-mortem evaluation of its electoral defeat, the UDP concluded that it had weak candidate appeal but a strong economic record.
The UDP immediately began attacking the government for its economic
policies, claiming that the new PUP budget showed no vision and con-
tained no specific measures to "alleviate the lot of the poor." The budget,
charged Dean Barrow, confirms the government's "absolute betrayal of
its manifesto to 'restore national dignity.'" While not disavowing its own
neoliberal orientation, the UDP attacked the economic policies approved
by the PUP, such as Export-Processing Zones and a foreign ship registry,
as "radically capitalist."[15]

Internal party factionalism has continued to plague the UDP during the PUP government. In early 1992 the party voted to expel the
party faction led by Derek Aikman and Hubert Elrington. These
party militants had broken with UDP leaders Manuel Esquivel and
Dean Barrow over the party's support for the proposed settlement of
the Guatemala-Belize dispute. Bipartisan support for the proposed
settlement indicated a new level of political maturity in Belize, for
which Esquivel and Barrow deserved credit. But their efforts in support of the settlement opened a new rift in their party and risked
their own leadership positions.

Upon expulsion, Aikman and Elrington formed the Patriotic Alliance for Territorial Integrity and a new party called the National Alliance for Belizean Rights. The Patriotic Alliance, a diehard
nationalistic faction, attracted the support of patriarch Philip Goldson and stirred up opposition to the Maritime Areas Bill (see Foreign
Policy). In addition to leadership differences on this foreign policy issue, the 1992 split reflected longtime divisions between the party's
NIP/National Party roots and the more modernizing elements of the
party led by the Liberal Party faction and by Dean Barrow. Although
Esquivel and Barrow were on the same side in the Patriotic Alliance
dispute, they each seek to be the party leader and a contest between
them could further split the party.

The UDP's base of support comes mainly from the NIP, which
historically was tied to elements of the upper and middle classes that
had a perceived interest in maintaining the colonial system. Although

it was initially identified with colonial interests and with the creole civil service, the NIP gradually reached out to the *mestizo* and Mayan communities. Since its founding in 1973 the UDP has become more of a national party, encompassing all classes and ethnic groups although a creole bias remains in party politics and policies. In contrast to the PUP, the UDP has a more structured and functioning party bureaucracy, perhaps because its leadership is not so tied to one figure. Although there is more internal party democracy within the UDP, like the PUP it lacks a firm rank-and-file membership and support base, with most organizing occurring just prior to elections.

In the political arena, the UDP is a center-right party that stands to the right of the PUP. It has been an outspoken critic of communism and an ardent proponent of free enterprise and the free market. Internationally the UDP is affiliated with the International Democratic Union, a global coalition of conservative parties with strong influence and financing from the U.S. Republican Party and the U.S. government.[16] The *People's Pulse* is the official newspaper of the UDP.

People's United Party

From the mid-1950s to 1984 PUP politics in Belize were dominated by one man, George Cadle Price, a middle-class Catholic creole. After returning to Belize from the United States where he had studied for the priesthood in the 1930s, Price entered politics, running first for the Belize City Council in 1943. Price soon became a leader of the incipient independence movement, which the colonial government at first considered subversive and dangerous.

In 1949 Price helped form the People's Committee to lead the fight against devaluation of the British Honduras dollar, and in 1950 this ad hoc committee became the PUP political party. The party was not an outgrowth of the colonial political system but represented social sectors intent on replacing the system. Self-government and adult suffrage were its principal political objectives.

In its early years the PUP relied heavily on both the national infrastructure and activism of the General Workers Union (GWU). In the 1954 election, for example, the PUP district candidates were local GWU leaders. Without the support offered by the labor movement, the successes of the PUP in the 1950s and 1960s would not have been possible. On the other hand, this very link to a political party with middle-class leadership served to undermine the independence and strength of the early labor movement by greatly moderating its progressive orientation.

In its beginning, the PUP was more of a popular movement, albeit directed by middle-class leaders, than a political party. With a firm base in the independence and labor movements, the PUP was also seen as the popular representative of most of society's disenfranchised sectors. But after becoming an accepted participant in the political system—especially following the British government's announcement of "full internal self-government" for British Honduras in 1963—the PUP lost its close alliances with the popular sectors. The party became an electoral machine with a personalized and paternalistic style of leadership that was out of touch with a changing society.[17] It evolved from a popular movement to a centrist political party that administered government in Belize for three decades, winning all general elections until 1984 (1954, 1957, 1961, 1969, 1974, and 1979).

After a major split in the party in 1956, George Price became the undisputed head of the PUP, and he went about building a party machine with members who owed him their personal loyalty. Largely as a function of this *personalismo*, the PUP has historically lacked a functioning bureaucracy and has not even had a paid general secretary, relying instead on a coterie of longtime party stalwarts guided by Price.[18] Following the coming of self-government in the mid-1960s, the center of power shifted from the party's loose internal structure to the government itself. The center of party power was the Cabinet, where Price was the undisputed chief.[19]

The lack of internal party democracy and an almost nonexistent party structure have long been contentious issues within the PUP. Spurred by Assad Shoman, V.H. Courtenay, and Said Musa, the PUP adopted a revised constitution in 1975 designed to increase party democracy and rank-and-file participation in the party. Although regarded as a victory for the rank-and-file and the party's progressive wing, the new provisions of the constitution were never recognized or enforced by Price and the dominant conservative leadership. Their response to demands for greater democracy within the PUP was that such changes would splinter the party at the very time when the country was nearing independence. Attempts to enforce the ignored constitution were labeled subversive.

The drive to open up the party and implement the democracy-enhancing measures of the 1975 constitution continued after independence and led to bitter infighting between the party's progressive and conservative factions. In fact, the demand for greater internal party democracy was expanded to include a call for increased popular participation in government in general. In a striking departure from protocol, two government ministers, Shoman and Musa, issued a public proclamation in 1982 advocating "steps to strengthen and deepen democracy in Belize." The two left-of-center leaders declared that "the democratic forms that we have inherited are clearly not adequate to deal with the present crisis. . . . It is not enough to say that the people are represented in the House of Representatives; as it presently functions and will undoubtedly continue to function, that institution can play no creative or dynamic role to ensure people's participation or to present alternatives as solutions to our problems."

This public criticism sparked the formation in Belize City of a party faction called the Democratic Direction. This faction contended that "the most fundamental problem is that democracy is not practiced in the party," and charged that "over a period of several decades, party organization and political education have been grossly underdeveloped."[20]

But beyond having a general interest in promoting party democracy, the Democratic Direction faction also wanted to unseat party chairperson Louis Sylvestre, chief spokesperson for the PUP's conservative faction. Responding to the Democratic Direction charges, Sylvestre attacked the faction and accused party ministers Shoman and Musa of being "communists." With Price promoting Sylvestre and fellow conservative Florencio Marin as the main party leaders, party progressives and rank-and-file militants became ever more marginalized. This infighting, combined with growing disenchantment over the ingrained autocratic style of the party, contributed to the PUP's defeat in the Belize City Council elections in 1983 and its stunning loss to the UDP in the 1984 general elections.

After supporting the PUP for 30 years as the governing party, Belizean voters were ready for a change in 1984. Independence had raised voters' expectations for a more rapid pace of economic development and three years of recessionary economic conditions (1981-84) turned voters away from the PUP. But the dissatisfaction with the PUP was not just a matter of economics. Belizeans were also tired of the one-man leadership of George Price and the PUP's lack of new blood.

Campaigning on the popular slogan "Belizeans First," the PUP squeaked back into power in the September 1989 election, winning by a swing vote of about 5 percent. The electoral shift back to the PUP was confirmed by the party's subsequent sweep of all nine seats of the Belize City Council. The PUP's successful challenge was based on the contention that the country had become more repressive and corrupt under the UDP. Appealing to nationalist sentiments, candidate Price charged that the UDP had opened the doors to foreign speculators and that Belizeans were not benefiting from new investment projects—as evidenced by a persistently high unemployment rate.[21]

Ideology of Price and the PUP

Known for his spartan and reclusive habits, George Price, 73, is widely respected for his honesty, integrity, and incorruptibility. He is a formidable politician, who has dedicated his life to the PUP and Belizean politics and is highly regarded for his ability as a party manager and skill at unifying disparate regional and ideological factions. While these talents have kept him at the top of the PUP hierarchy, his tight control over the party has discouraged the emergence of younger leaders who would appeal to new generations of voters. Considered the "father of the nation" by most Belizeans, Price is also seen as a relic of the colonial era. Given his stamina for politics, questions about who would replace Price as party leader have been pushed aside. But clearly waiting in the wings are Said Musa and Florencio Marin, both longtime party militants with their own personal following.

The PUP is a centrist party with no clearly defined ideological principles and with no firm international affiliations. Under Price's leadership, the PUP has become a truly national organization, bringing together all the country's diverse ethnic groups and classes under its blue-and-white party colors. Guided by Price's own centrist and moderate tendencies, the party rejects both "atheistic communism" and "unbridled capitalism," advocating instead a policy of "wise capitalism."

The PUP has long advocated the development of a stronger local capitalist class and close economic ties with the United States, which it calls the "natural ally" of Belize.[22] The U.S. flag was even flown at many early PUP rallies. Although allied with labor during his early political career, Price has from the beginning regarded leftist or militant labor leadership with suspicion.

At the same time, PUP policies have a persistent social democratic tone as reflected in its party constitution, which calls for "economic democracy" and "stimulating higher economic productivity through planned development of the nation's resources for the benefit of all the people." Furthermore, the party constitution states that every Belizean should receive "a fair share of the national wealth." This social democratic philosophy was also evident in the government's "1990-1994 Development Plan." Presented by Said Musa, whose portfolio includes Economic Development, the plan observes: "Economic growth on its own does not guarantee people-centered development as witnessed by the fact that social well-being has lagged behind. The urgent task at hand is to raise income and productivity for sustainable growth while also securing human development and social equality for all."[23]

Although basically a centrist party with an elitist structure, the PUP has constantly been tugged toward more progressive positions by its left-of-center leaders and militants.[24] For the most part, however, progressive policies remain rhetorical flourishes while government budgeting and programming reveal the party's more conservative nature.

Despite its long history and impressive successes, the PUP has no real dues-membership system or grassroots structure. After the 1984 defeat, it did go through a reorganization led by Florencio Marin that formalized regional committees such as the northern PUP contingent in Orange Walk and Corozal. Yet the party still has no organized rank-and-file base or outreach program, relying instead on its control of government and the leadership of George Price to ensure its perpetuity. Functioning as the voice of the party is the *Belize Times*, which like the PUP headquarters is located on property owned by the Price estate.

The PUP in Power: 1989-92

At the start of its 1989-94 term, the government's maneuvering room was limited as never before by a strong parliamentary opposition—placing a premium on party unity. Because of this, every elected PUP representative was given a role in a ministry, either as a full minister or deputy.[25] With one UDP representative crossing the aisle to the ruling party immediately after the 1989 general elections, the PUP's tenuous control of government was strengthened.

The PUP did little to waver from conservative economic policies put in place in the 1980s. Many hallmarks of the UDP administration—tight budgetary control, export promotion, encouragement of foreign investment, and close cooperation with the private sector—were continued under the PUP. Although there were no sharp shifts in economic policy, PUP rhetoric was markedly different. Declarations of faith in the free market and foreign investment were toned down and modified by statements about the need for shared development to benefit the entire society, particularly the unemployed, women, and youth.

Among specific PUP campaign promises in 1989 were the following:

– Disbandment of the Security Intelligence Service (SIS) police unit.

– Nationalization of the University College of Belize and severance of ties with Ferris State (see Schools and Education).

– Reduced role for U.S. advisers (see U.S. Economic Aid) and greater presence of Commonwealth technical assistance.

– Renewed restrictions on sale of Belizean property to foreigners.

— Increased attention to government provision of housing, education, and health services.

— Increased local production of food and new land reform efforts.

— Creation of a semi-independent statutory committee to regulate television and radio broadcasting, encourage local TV programming, and grant private radio licenses.

— Discontinued sales of Belizean passports.[26]

Immediately upon regaining power, the PUP government abolished the UDP-established SIS secret police unit, reduced the government's control over the media (see Communications Media), and abolished the law that made libel a criminal offense. The sale of Belizean passports was curtailed but the practice essentially continued under a government program to attract new foreign investment, particularly from Asia. In taking these measures, the PUP fulfilled a number of its campaign promises while establishing a more open and social democratic direction for government. But the conservative financial policies of the UDP government were retained, prohibiting spending on health care, social services, and other public investment in the common welfare from rising to meet the expanding needs of an increasing population.

Although the PUP did implement many of its campaign promises, the new government also adopted policies and programs for which it had previously criticized the UDP. For example, when in opposition, the PUP had cautioned the UDP government against the establishment of Export-Processing Zones (EPZs). It also complained that the UDP allowed U.S. military engineers on a bridge-building exercise to establish a "beachhead" in the country. As the ruling party, however, the PUP approved legislation authorizing EPZs and invited U.S. military engineers, this time accompanied by 25 army medics, back to the country to repair the bridge.

Foreign Policy

Although Belize has been independent only since 1981, the experience of government leaders in international relations extends back to the early 1960s. During the period of self-government, Britain retained control over the management of foreign affairs but allowed the PUP administration to participate actively in the country's foreign policy initiatives.

The pre-independence government projected a progressive foreign policy linking Belize with other national liberation movements and with efforts to restructure North-South trading relations. This left-of-center foreign policy orientation was understandable for a country trying to win international support for its independence and came naturally at a time when Michael Manley was prime minister in Jamaica, Jimmy Carter was the U.S. president, and Omar Torrijos was president in Panama. Belize became a prominent member of the Movement of Non-Aligned Nations, and the PUP even seriously considered joining the Socialist International.[27]

Since achieving independence, Belize has been more circumspect and conservative about its foreign policy positions. It cannot afford distancing itself from either the United States (on which it increasingly depends for trade and aid) or Britain (which maintains 1,500 troops on its soil). In addition to these diplomatic considerations, Belize has increasingly used foreign policy as an instrument to bolster trade and investment. In this way, the direction of foreign policymaking in Belize is not unlike that of most other nations in the 1990s, with economic considerations dominating international relations.

The foreign policy of Belize has been largely determined by its economic, political, and military links with the United States and Britain, and its geographical ties to both Central America and the Caribbean. British influence in Belize has been on the decline for the last several decades, but Belize's foreign policy continues to be affected by its membership in the Commonwealth of Nations and its dependence on British military protection. In the 1980s the United States came to play a more influential role in the definition of the country's foreign policy. The official foreign policy has been one of nonalignment, while, as George Price noted in 1984, "recognizing our special ties with the United States."[28] Increasingly, though, it has been the country's own economic interests in securing trade and investment that have guided the foreign policy of Belize.

The nation's independence in 1981 and the growing political crisis in Central America in the early 1980s combined to open the doors to large flows of economic aid to Belize and to a marked increase in U.S. strategic and diplomatic interest in the country. The inclusion of Belize in the Caribbean Basin Initiative (CBI) drew the country closer to the U.S. concept of economic and political development.[29] In 1989 the new PUP government promised to continue Belize's "special relationship" with the United States while forging new and similar ties with other industrialized countries.

Belize has historically attempted to maintain a certain independence from U.S. foreign policy goals. In its push for independence, Belize counted on the support of the Movement of Non-Aligned Nations. Among the firmest supporters of Belizean independence were Cuba, Panama, Nicaragua, and Mexico. Although eager to receive increased aid in the 1980s, the country was leery of being drawn too close to the U.S. military build-up in the region, fearing that it could easily be sucked into the regional conflict. The Esquivel administration appointed an ambassador for the region, including Nicaragua, while declining to endorse U.S. efforts to oust Panama's General Manuel Noriega. In turn, the PUP administration likewise withheld its endorsement of the U.S. invasion of Panama.

As economic concerns have become paramount, Belize's foreign policy has taken a decidedly pragmatic tone, as evidenced by its decision to accept Cuban assistance in the form of medical teams. This pragmatic emphasis was readily apparent during the tenure of Foreign Minister Dean Barrow, and is equally true of the PUP government. In its 1989 party manifesto the PUP declared that Belize "should see the world as the world is and not according to ideology. This constitutes a realistic approach."

Belize in the Region

A popular conception of the country's role in the region is embodied in the slogan of the nation's radio station: Radio Belize is the "Caribbean beat in the heart of Central America." In the late 1950s the PUP opposed British efforts to include the colony in the Federation of the West Indies because the nationalist leaders saw the regional plan as a colonial strategy to continue British control while blocking Belize's future development as a Central American country.[30]

Drawn culturally to the Commonwealth Caribbean and with its right to self-determination not respected by Central American nations, Belize joined the Caribbean Community (Caricom). Although Caricom membership brought only limited economic benefits, it did serve to further the country's drive for independence. Under the Esquivel government, Belize showed little interest in deepening its ties to the Caribbean. The UDP administration pulled back from an initial threat to withdraw from Caricom and announced in 1986 that it was fully committed to the economic body. Yet the government noted "at times we question the level of benefits that accrue to our individual countries through intraregional arrangements that were perhaps more ambitious in their conception than in their execution."[31]

Belize has historically been excluded from Central American regional accords. It played no direct role in the Central America peace process due both to its traditional self-imposed isolation from Central American politics and to certain opposition from Guatemala if Belize had pushed for inclusion in the process.[32] But since the late 1980s Belize has been recognized by its isthmus neighbors as a bona fide Central American nation. Belize now attends regional presidential summits and has been invited to join the Central American Parliament (Parlacen) and the renovated Central American Common Market. For its part, the private sector through the Chamber of Commerce and Industry participates in the region's U.S.-supported regional chamber of commerce.

Belize has historically enjoyed good relations with Mexico. Unlike other countries of Central America, in Belize there is a positive popular perception of Mexico and Mexican society. In recent years this positive relationship has been shored up by a number of new trade, aid, and cultural exchange accords. Closer relations have also been established with Venezuela, another oil-producing nation, which sought Belize's support for its full membership in Caricom. One of the first foreign policy victories of the post-1989 PUP administration was its entry in January 1991 as the 35th member of the Organization of American States (OAS).

The Dispute with Guatemala

Beginning with its independence from Spain in 1821, Guatemala claimed the territory of British Honduras as its own. It was not until August 1991, on the eve of Belize's tenth anniversary of independence, that Guatemala recognized the country's right to self-determination and independence. The so-called Anglo-Guatemalan dispute went through hot and cold periods during British colonial rule. Following the granting of self-government to the colony in the early 1960s and as Belize sought its independence, tensions intensified and the conflict gained international attention.

It was Guatemala's position that when it gained independence it also inherited control over that section of Belize governed by the Guatemalan province of the Spanish empire. Using the same logic, Mexico claimed that part of Belize bordering the Yucatán, which composed part of colonial Mexico's jurisdiction. Britain, however, dismissed these claims, arguing that neither Guatemala nor Mexico had ever occupied Belize. It also cited a 1786 British-Spanish treaty that permitted British settlements while recognizing Spanish sovereignty. The defeat of a Spanish naval attack in 1798—known and still commemorated in Belize as the Battle of St. George's Caye—lent new weight to the British claim over the territory, which was subsequently treated as a quasi colony.

Further confirming the British claim was the Anglo-Guatemalan Treaty of 1859 which set the boundaries "between the Republic and the British Settlement and Possessions in the Bay of Honduras." Britain and Guatemala signed a new convention to the treaty in 1863 under which Britain agreed to provide funds for the construction of a road from Guatemala City to the country's Atlantic Coast. But Guatemala, then at war with El Salvador, did not ratify the convention in the specified time, allowing it to lapse. For the next several decades Guatemala tried without success to have the convention renewed. In the end, it was the British position that the 1859 treaty was not an agreement of cession on the part of Guatemala but one in which Guatemala recognized the existing boundaries of British Honduras, which had been officially declared a crown colony in 1862. For its part, Guatemala based its claims to Belize on the British failure to pay for the road to the sea and hence the invalidity of the 1859 treaty. For its part, the Mexican government by the 1880s had ceased to assert its territorial rights over the northern section of the British colony.

The conflict lay dormant until the early 1930s when the British attempted to arrange a joint boundary survey of the territory, at which time Guatemala declined to cooperate and renewed its land claims. The 1945 Guatemalan constitution even referred to Belize as the 23rd department of the country.[33]

Negotiations to settle what was called the Anglo-Guatemalan dispute resumed in 1961, but with Belize's elected representatives playing no role in the talks. In that same year George Price, serving as the country's first prime minister, secured associate member status for Belize with the United Nations Economic Commission for Latin America (ECLA), marking the effective beginning of the PUP's own campaign to win international recognition of Belize's right to self-determination. In 1962 a new series of talks began—this time with Belizeans as observers. But Guatemala repeatedly broke off talks, threatened invasion, and increased its territorial claims. In 1965 Guatemala and Britain agreed to have a U.S. attorney, appointed by President Lyndon Johnson, mediate the dispute. The U.S. mediator in 1968 proposed a draft treaty that, while declaring that Belize would gain independence in 1970, would have given Guatemala effective control over Belize. This proposal was soundly rejected by the Belizean people, and Philip Goldson won fame for his strong denunciation of the United States for being "heavily committed to Guatemala."

The Two-Treaty Package, 1969-72

Beginning in 1969 negotiations resumed around discussions of a "two-treaty package."[34] This included a proposed treaty of recognition by Guatemala and Britain (and in the Belizean proposal also by Mexico, the United States, and Canada) and a treaty of cooperation between Belize and Guatemala in matters of commerce, agriculture, defense, and foreign affairs. So optimistic was Prime Minister Price that he predicted that independence would be achieved by 1972. The threat of an invasion of Belize by Guatemalan and Salvadoran forces and the resulting massive deployment of British troops increased tensions and caused a near breakdown in negotiations in 1972.[35]

Internationalization of Support, 1975-80

Guatemala again broke off negotiations in 1975 after Belize appealed for UN support. Talks resumed afresh in 1976, continuing on and off for the next four years. Guatemala persisted in its claim for Belizean territory, although gradually reducing the size of the demand, while Belize, bolstered by UN resolutions, replied that not one bit of Belizean territory would be ceded. In 1975 the pro-independence movement failed to garner the backing of any Latin American nations except Cuba. But with the support of Panama's Omar Torrijos in 1976 momentum began building in Latin America for Belizean independence.

Encouraged by its hemispheric advocates, Belize began a concerted diplomatic drive to gain world support for its independence. The strategy was one of "parallel roads" to achieving independence— on the one hand supporting negotiations to convince Guatemala to drop its claims, while on the other hand working to secure an effective international guarantee that would allow Belize to become independent despite Guatemala's continued hostility. At the same time, the Belizean government promoted the concept of "territorial integrity" in such international arenas as the UN and the Organization of American States in an effort to counteract suggestions from the United States and Britain that it cede some of its territory to Guatemala. By withholding the promise of maintaining a British garrison in Belize after independence, Britain hoped to pressure Belizean leaders into agreeing to cede part of its territory to facilitate the negotiations. Guatemala was demanding about a quarter of Belizean territory.

Conceding that negotiations with Guatemala remained stalled, the PUP government decided to increase its efforts to gain international support, especially through favorable UN resolutions. This initiative was hindered by strong opposition from the UDP, which rejected the idea of independence without settling with Guatemala and thereby risking a Guatemalan attack. Initially Britain also attempted to discourage the new international campaign but eventually agreed to support the effort. The PUP's drive to gain the backing of the UN General Assembly proved crucial, resulting in six favorable resolutions between 1975 and 1980, each one gaining additional support. The resolutions affirmed the right of Belize to seek independence and, significantly, declared that the territorial integrity of Belize must be respected.

It was not, however, until 1980 that all key elements were in place for the transition to independence, with U.S. approval of the 1980 UN resolution proving highly significant. The 1980 resolution included a few new provisions that facilitated the implementation of independence, including a statement that Belize would be declared independent before the next session, that Britain and Guatemala would continue negotiations, and that Britain would be urged to "continue to ensure the security and territorial integrity of Belize." Independence at last seemed certain, and in December 1980 Britain announced the convening of a conference to draft a new constitution for an independent Belize.

Heads of Agreement, 1981

The first eight months of 1981 proved to be a highly charged time in Belize. Although independence seemed certain, Britain still declined to provide a defense guarantee, insisting that even greater efforts must be undertaken to achieve a peaceful settlement with Guatemala. After brief talks in February and March, the three negotiating parties—Britain, Guatemala, and Belize—signed a document on March 11, 1981, called the "Heads of Agreement" or "Bases de Entendimiento." The agreement stipulated the terms of a possible treaty that would be ironed out in future negotiations and then implemented.

As set out in the agreement, in return for the recognition of an independent Belize and dropping all land claims, Guatemala would be granted "permanent and unimpeded access" to the sea from Puerto Barrios (Guatemala's Caribbean port) through Belizean waters as well as the nonmilitary use of two cayes in those waters (the uninhabited Ranguana and Sapodilla cayes). Under the terms of the accord, Belize would agree to give Guatemala free port facilities, seabed mining rights, and certain territorial access privileges (including the construction of an oil pipeline across its territory). The document specified, however, that "nothing in these provisions shall prejudice any rights or interests of Belize or the Belizean people." As such, the agreement was a major diplomatic advance for Belize.

The 16 points of the Heads of Agreement were largely face-saving devices for Guatemala after having dropped its land claims. In both Guatemala and Belize the Heads of Agreement provoked strong reaction. The rightist National Liberation Movement (MLN) in Guatemala called it a sellout and pressured the government to withdraw from the negotiations. Riots broke out in Belize City, Orange Walk, and Dangriga to protest the accord, which was interpreted by many opposition leaders as a violation of Belizean sovereignty and territorial integrity. To a large degree, the riots were politically inspired by elements within the UDP, which had consistently opposed independence without a British defense guarantee. Joining the attack against government were the short-lived Belize Action Movement and the Anti-Communist Society.

Yet the riots represented more than political maneuvering and opportunistic organizing. The violent upheaval also reflected the deep popular concern that independence would open the country to a Guatemalan invasion. There existed strong sentiment that Belize should not have to compromise its territorial integrity in any way to gain its independence. This mixture of confusion, fear, and unwillingness to compromise sparked the protest which resulted in one death and many injuries. As O. Nigel Bolland observed, the racism and slander that characterized the protests "represented the nadir of politically motivated violence and abuse in Belize."[36]

The Heads of Agreement was subject to widely varying interpretations in Guatemala and Belize which led to a breakdown in the negotiations in July 1981. Only at that time did Britain agree to maintain a military presence in Belize "for an appropriate period" to guarantee its defense. With that guarantee in place, Belizeans viewed more favorably the post-independence prospects of the country.

Independent Belize, 1981-90

Negotiations between Guatemala and Belize remained stalled for most of the first decade of Belizean independence. Belize sought economic and cultural cooperation with Guatemala while, at least during the PUP administrations, attempting to resolve the dispute under the provisions outlined in the Heads of Agreement. Worries about a Guatemalan invasion were allayed by the firm commitment of Britain to maintain its garrison and jet fighters. A preliminary set of principles for an accord between the two countries was circulated in 1990 under which Guatemala would recognize Belize's existing border claims while Belize would limit its international sea boundary to three miles at its southernmost point, thereby ensuring Guatemala easy access to the Atlantic Coast.

Independence Recognized and Sea Access Debated, 1991-2

A month prior to the tenth anniversary of Belizean independence, Guatemala's President Jorge Serrano announced that Guatemala was recognizing Belize's right to self-determination and sovereignty. That announcement and a later one in September that Guatemala had recognized the independence of Belize were the products of ongoing negotiations between Guatemalan diplomats and a bipartisan Belizean delegation. Apparently Guatemala finally agreed to recognize the independence of Belize on the condition that it would gain expanded sea rights off Belize's southern coast.

The announcement upset the media and right wing in Guatemala, whose pressure convinced Serrano to cancel a planned state visit to Belize. In Belize, like in Guatemala, news of the progress of the negotiations sparked some dissent. Rather than calming fears in Belize about Guatemala, the announcement of Guatemala's recognition of Belizean independence opened up the old internal political controversy over what Belize should do, if anything, to meet Guatemala's demand to permanent access to the Caribbean Sea. There also existed the conviction that the bipartisan commission was attempting to push through a final settlement without adequately informing or consulting the populace.

When the Price government announced that it was prepared, as a result of bipartisan negotiations, to limit its sea territory to three miles in southern Belize to give Guatemala secure passage to the high seas through its own territorial waters, the response was a wave of popular dissension. As defined in the Maritime Areas Bill, which the PUP government sponsored and passed, Belize agreed to extend its territorial sea to the internationally acceptable 12 miles although limiting it to three miles south of the Sarstoon River. It remained unclear whether this three-mile territorial sea would then become Belize's sea boundary.

Initially the bill counted on the support of the opposition UDP, but this was withdrawn in response to strong dissent within the party to the bipartisan position advocated by UDP leaders Esquivel and Barrow. For its part, the PUP government attempted to counteract popular opposition with a "Give Peace a Chance" popular education and publicity campaign to explain the importance of passing the bill and ending the long dispute, even if it would mean that Belize would make a small concession of sea territory. According to the bill and if approved by the electorate, Belize would give Guatemala more than the legally required right of "innocent passage" but would actually cede its own rights to sea territory.

According to the Guatemalan constitution and understood by the Belizean government, any final agreement to the territorial claims will be subject to popular referendums. In Guatemala, however, sentiment that "Belice es Nuestro" (Belize is Ours) runs deep because of so much previous government propaganda to that effect. In Belize, popular opinion runs deep against any settlement in which Belize cedes anything to Guatemala, even sea rights that it has not previously used. Widespread distrust of Guatemala persists in Belize, and many fear the consequences of the future departure of British troops. Elements within the opposition continue to use the Guatemala dispute in a demagogic and opportunistic way to attack the PUP and stir up nationalistic and racial fears of a takeover by the "Spanish."

For any final resolution to Guatemala's claims for secure and unimpeded access through the sea, the PUP government will need to improve its educational efforts while renewing bipartisan support for a final treaty. But given the depth of popular sentiment against any cession of sea rights and the political liabilities of supporting any such compromise, a bipartisan position on the issue might be difficult to secure. Although Guatemala did indeed recognize the independence of Belize—a position it cannot back away from under international law—it is in the economic interests of both nations to resolve the remaining issues amicably so that joint development projects can be pursued. A final agreement with Guatemala would also facilitate the integration of Belize into the Central American economic and political community.

Business Comes First

Aside from the negotiations with Guatemala, the issue of free trade has been the salient foreign policy concern. Belize worries that trade liberalization initiatives, such as the proposed North American Free Trade Agreement (NAFTA) and the Enterprise for the Americas Initiative, will result in the dismantling of the Caribbean Basin Initiative (CBI) and the sugar import-quota system, both of which give the country privileged access to the U.S. market. Belize is similarly concerned that it will soon lose its privileged position in the European market, established under the Lomé Convention.

Belize has not openly rejected the new free trade initiatives on the part of the United States, but in any future negotiations it wants to protect its current trade position. Jointly with the other Caricom members, Belize entered into a "framework agreement" on trade liberalization with Washington in 1991. The common opinion in the Caribbean was that the free trade train was coming, like it or not, and it behooved them to join the negotiations rather than being left behind. At least initially the framework agreement is being negotiated on a regional basis rather than bilaterally between individual nations and the United States, but considering the fragile unity of the Caricom countries this regional approach may break down.

All the Caribbean nations, like those of Central America, insist on the need for gradualism in trade liberalization. They want the principle of "relative reciprocity" to be respected on the grounds that they are unequal partners because of their small undeveloped economies. Belizean manufacturers are unable to compete with their much larger counterparts, whether in the United States or in countries such as Mexico or Brazil. Rather than simultaneously dropping all tariff and nontariff barriers, Belize would prefer a schedule of progressive liberalization that gives its local producers a much longer implementation period.

Security Forces

The Belize Defense Force (BDF), formed in 1978, resulted from the merger of the Police Special Forces and the Belize Volunteer Guard. It includes an army of about 750 soldiers (including a couple of female platoons), a Maritime Wing with 50 marines and four patrol boats, and a 15-member Air Wing with two transport planes. In addition, there is a reserve and a volunteer component of the BDF that add another 500 members. Defense receives about 6 percent of the government's current accounts budget, more than the 5 percent allocated to Social Security and Welfare but less than the 17-20 percent allocated to education or the 8 percent for health.[37]

The BDF receives aid and training from Britain, the United States, and Canada, and has been commanded by British officers under the British Loan Service Commandant program. Soon after returning to office, the PUP government assigned direct control of the BDF to a Belizean officer. In 1990 the first Belizean was appointed to be chief of staff at the Ministry of Defense. The BDF's officer corps includes a dozen or more officers on loan from the British armed forces.[38] In the United States, BDF officers are trained at Fort Benning while others receive jungle warfare training at U.S. bases in Panama.

The BDF's main base is at the Price Barracks near the international airport. Among its main operations are joint border surveillance with British troops, anti-drug-smuggling activities, defense of the international airport, and assistance to police forces in such areas as search-and-rescue and immigration control.

The 500-member Belize Police Force (BPF) is the country's main civilian police unit. It is a low-paid, disorganized, and loosely disciplined force that is widely dismissed as being ineffective in such basic matters as crime fighting and traffic control.

Beginning in the mid-1980s the BDF and the BPF became increasingly involved in antinarcotics operations. At the 1991 annual

BDF training program, Belizean troops together with the British Forces Belize conducted an exercise in which these forces intervened in a fictitious republic following a call from that country's president to help apprehend "narco-guerrillas" who had occupied the country.[39] The BDF routinely assists police as well as immigration and customs departments in search-and-rescue operations and drug eradication efforts. Beginning in 1991 BDF troops were also appointed "special constables" to aid police in fighting urban crime.

Human Rights

Human rights violations are not the major concern in Belize that they are in most other Central American countries. There have been no reports, for example, of politically motivated killings or disappearances. Freedom of speech and assembly are not only tolerated but form part of the political culture.[40] In marked contrast to its neighbors, police are occasionally convicted and sentenced for abuses. The new PUP government in 1989 further contributed to the improved human rights climate by reducing government control over the media, abolishing the semiclandestine Security Intelligence Service (SIS), and adopting a more tolerant position regarding Central American immigrants. Human rights monitors also find the PUP administration to be more accessible than the UDP government.

Nevertheless, serious concerns continue to exist, including the lack of labor protection, persistent police brutality, inadequate prison conditions, discriminatory treatment of Central American immigrants, and the violation of women's rights (see Women and Feminism; Labor and Unions).[41] Before it was abolished, for example, the SIS and other police were known to subject political dissidents and community activists to harassment and interrogation.[42] Reflecting a widespread fear that the country would be flooded with Spanish-speaking Central Americans, police abuses were particularly common against refugees and other Central Americans in 1987 and 1988 (see Immigration and Emigration). The human rights climate in regard to Central American immigrants significantly improved after 1988, and the government has launched new programs to integrate the immigrants into Belizean society.

Although police brutality and discrimination against Central American immigrants are not as widespread as they once were, Salvadorans and Guatemalans living in Belize are still subject to harassment, unequal treatment, and mass deportations. In nighttime raids, police collect people without documents and deport them without hearings. For example, in 1990 a Guatemalan was arrested, allegedly tortured, and then deported to Guatemala, with the police claiming that he was a member of a Guatemalan guerrilla organization. Because many of them are not legal residents, employers frequently deny the immigrants their proper pay. The government is also slow to grant work permits, social security papers, and other documentation needed by refugees and migrant workers.

The founding in December 1987 of the Human Rights Commission of Belize (HRCB) has been an important factor in raising public awareness about human rights. This independent nonprofit organization has produced a basic human rights manual and has initiated a human rights training course that has been incorporated into the curriculum for police cadets. According to William "Billy" Heusner, an officer of the Human Rights Commission, police brutality is an intensifying problem in Belize. Urban youth in Belize City often fall victim to excessive police violence, with complaints registered against the police rising in 1990 and 1991. A government decision authorized uniformed BDF members to begin patrolling city streets with the police in an attempt to crack down on rising crime, a decision the HRCB criticized. Heusner and other critics suggest that Belize increase its police force and begin dismantling its army rather than mixing police and military functions.[43]

Another continuing human rights problem is the unequal access to legal assistance. Lawyers in Belize frequently secure acquittals on the basis of improperly gathered testimony—an outcome rarely attained by poor Belizeans without the funds to hire a lawyer. According to Heusner, the country's legal aid office is still not very effective and magistrates tend to believe the police more often than the accused when there is no lawyer for the defense.[44]

After a fact-finding tour by a bipartisan committee of the National Assembly, constitutional guarantees respecting the right to be informed of charges and the right to legal counsel are now prominently displayed in all 60 police stations. Although there have been some improvements in this area of legal rights, the rise of drug-related crime and theft in Belize City has swamped the country's judicial and prison systems. The police are so notoriously slow in presenting evidence against those charged that many prisoners are incarcerated for several months until their cases are heard, with bail bonds set at unreasonably high levels.

Originally built to hold 89 prisoners, the Belize City Prison held 387 inmates in early 1992. Prisoners are crowded into small cells, where five or six sleep on cardboard sheets laid down on cement floors. Windows are completely open, with no protection against rain, cold, or insects. There are no toilets, only slop buckets, and there is no medical care for prisoners. The women are housed in cramped conditions, and because there are no educational, work, or training programs for them they remain locked up during most of their prison stay.[45]

A related concern is the rising invasion of privacy as part of a new police campaign against illegal drug use. In response to the alarming increase in drug trafficking and cocaine/crack use, the Misuse of Drug Law of 1990 gives police wider latitude in drug-related cases, specifically allowing arrests on evidence of "drug paraphernalia." Prohibitive bonds are being set for those found with such paraphernalia or small amounts of drugs, and many languish in prison for months before their cases are heard.

While human rights monitors in most other Central American nations and Mexico necessarily focus on issues of political repression and vigilante violence, human rights advocates in Belize interpret the concept of human rights as including respect for basic economic and social rights. The HRCB exhorts the government to more aggressively integrate youth and the unemployed into the economy, arguing that economic deprivation and the breakdown of the family are the main causes of the country's crime and drug problems. The Human Rights Commission is also active in promoting the concept of children's rights, charging that incest, child abuse, and child neglect are common in Belize.[46]

2

Economy

© Tom Barry

State of the Economy

Economically, independence came at a bad time for Belize. The People's United Party (PUP) had campaigned on a platform of "political and economic independence." It gained the former but was confronted by the hard and complicated reality of the independent nation's economic dependence. High oil prices, low sugar prices, and a recessionary world market in the early 1980s pushed the country to the edge of bankruptcy as foreign exchange reserves dried up and the government's budget deficit widened. At a point in 1983 when the government was hard put to meet its payroll and had only several weeks worth of foreign exchange left in the Central Bank, the International Monetary Fund (IMF) intervened with an emergency loan. That balance-of-payments support loan was followed by an IMF standby arrangement under which the government agreed to raise interest rates, rein in its budget, and impose a series of austerity measures, including tax increases and a public-sector wage freeze.

For the PUP, not only did independence come at an unfortunate economic moment—so did the 1984 elections. Burdened by a balance-of-payments crisis and a deficit-ridden budget, the PUP suffered a decisive electoral defeat in December 1984. The United Democratic Party (UDP) swept into Belmopan with an economic development rhetoric that stressed private initiative, free markets, and export promotion. The UDP also reaped the good fortune of taking over the government just as the international economic scene was improving. From 1981 through 1985, the economy fluctuated wildly, suffering some negative per capita GDP growth (Figure 2a). By 1986 the economy was showing clear signs of rebounding, with the 1986-90 period characterized by increased exports, rapid economic growth, rising investment, and increased tourism income. During those heady years the GDP registered an average annual increase of over 13 percent, dipping to about 5 percent in 1991. An infusion of U.S. bilateral funds also helped ease the balance-of-payments crisis and allowed the UDP government to balance its budget.[1]

The rosy economic picture painted by balance-of-payments and export statistics formed the salient feature of the UDP's "Stand Firm" campaign in 1989. To further sweeten the economic scene in an election year, the party offered the citizenry a series of tax-relief measures, a reduction in utility rates, and several public-sector construction projects.[2] Although the populace was pleased by steady economic growth, there was a widespread sense that little of the bene-

Figure 2a
Annual Per Capita GDP Growth

In percentage.

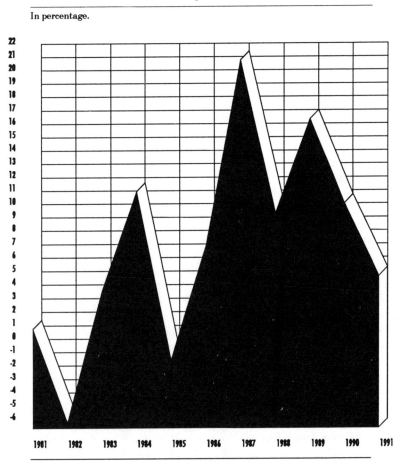

SOURCE: Office of Central Statistics, U.S. Embassy, Belize, February 1992.

fits had trickled down and that foreign investors were getting privileged treatment. Continued high unemployment rates, declining government services, and frustration with high indirect taxes were other economic factors contributing to the PUP's narrow victory in 1989.

The tourism boom and continuing increases in agroexports kept the economy on a roll through 1990, with real economic growth in that year registering 9 percent or more. But recession in the United States, the country's main trading partner and source of tourists, cut economic growth to the 3-5 percent range in 1991.

Although the rhetoric of the PUP administration has been markedly different from the neoliberal language adopted by the previous government, its economic policies have been much the same. The new administration has continued to promote agroexport production and tourism while maintaining tight fiscal management. The often divergent rhetoric of the two political parties has served to mask what have proved to be similar economic policies.

Economic Structure

Services—bolstered by the booming tourist industry—contribute more to the GDP than either primary or secondary productive activities. Primary activities, including agriculture, forestry, fishing, and to a much lesser extent mining, account for about 18 percent of the GDP, while the secondary sector of manufacturing, electricity and water, and construction represents about a quarter of the GDP (Figure 2b). When combined with the country's agroprocessing industries (such as citrus concentrate extraction), which are officially classified as part of the manufacturing sector, agriculture clearly still represents the most important economic activity in Belize. The combined agricultural sector accounts for as much as 25 percent of the GDP, 65-70 percent of export earnings, and 30-40 percent of employment.[3] Sugar is the country's leading export, followed by citrus, apparel, bananas, and seafood (Figure 2c). Among the most dynamic sectors in recent years have been tourism and the construction business.

Between 1986 and 1991 Belize enjoyed steady economic growth, distinguishing it from most Latin American countries. Another positive feature of the Belizean economy is that its $140 million foreign debt (1991) is the smallest in Central America—both in absolute terms and relative to export income. Unlike its less fortunate neighbors, a much higher portion of its debt—84 percent—is held by multilateral and bilateral institutions rather than by private bankers and creditors who demand higher rates of interest. Although debt has increased rapidly since 1984, Belize still has relatively low ratios of debt/GDP (36 percent) and debt service/export income (7 percent).[4]

Government tax revenues come primarily from taxes on international trade, mostly from imports. Duties are highest on finished consumer goods, lower on intermediate goods, and lowest or nonexistent on production inputs and capital goods.[5] These taxes raise more than 60 percent of all tax revenue. Property taxes are negligible in Belize, constituting just 1.5 percent of total tax revenues. Low tax rates are applied to undervalued land, and political connections often result in tax exemptions or deliberately low property assessments. Income taxes are also low, representing 22 percent of total tax revenue, and fall disproportionately on wage earners since deductions are taken directly from paychecks. Businesses, which must actually report income, find it easier to elude this economic bite. Levies on goods and services make up the balance of the country's tax revenue.

The tax structure in Belize is outdated, regressive, and in need of serious reform. Light taxation of property and disproportionate reliance on wage income levies as well as the many exemptions granted

Figure 2b
Leading Economic Sectors, 1991

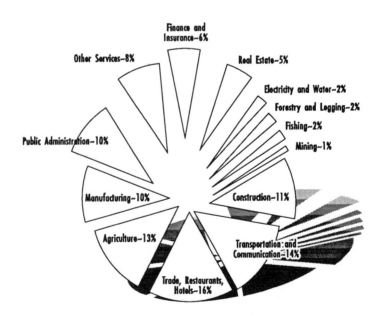

SOURCE: Office of Central Statistics, U.S. Embassy, Belize, February 1992.

to investors shift the tax burden away from those most able to afford it. As currently structured, taxes are unable to raise sufficient revenues to cover government expenses and responsibilities. In considering proposals for tax reform, the government will have to weigh the political costs of creating new taxes and increasing present ones against the need for more current revenue. It will also have to consider whether to make the system more progressive by increasing taxes on business income, property, and investment or to maintain the present regressive focus by increasing indirect taxes on consumption and services. As Belize is pushed to liberalize its trade regulations to correspond to free trade regimens, it will face increasing pressure to slash its duties and taxes on international trade. If it does cut tariffs, the government will likely seek more direct ways to tax consumption.

Figure 2c

Leading Exports, 1990

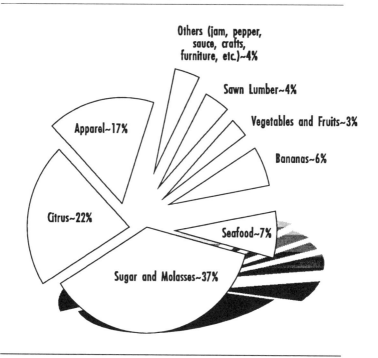

Others (jam, pepper, sauce, crafts, furniture, etc.)~4%

Sawn Lumber~4%

Vegetables and Fruits~3%

Bananas~6%

Apparel~17%

Citrus~22%

Seafood~7%

Sugar and Molasses~37%

SOURCES: U.S. Embassy, *Economic Trends: Belize*, December 1990; Central Statistical Office (Belmopan).

Dependency on Imports and Export Growth

Like many economies in the region, Belize's economy is characterized by its extreme openness, precarious external dependence, and small size. As a British colony, the country grew accustomed to importing virtually everything it consumed. Although the country now has its own small industrial sector and food production system, a heavy reliance on imports still characterizes the economy. As a result of all these imports—which range from U.S. wheat and Dutch condensed milk to electronic items and capital goods—Belize regularly suffers a large annual trade deficit.

The country's export income results from a small number of commodities. The top five export commodities (sugar, citrus concentrate, apparel, bananas, and seafood) represent 88 percent of total export income. Besides this dependency on a few items, another weakness in Belize's export production is that all its major export commodities are low-unit-value items, which generate less foreign exchange than the same volume of high-unit-value manufactured or highly processed goods.[6]

The country's trade deficit rose from $37 million in 1982 to $82 million in 1990 to $147 million in 1991. During the 1982-91 period, export income increased about 38 percent while imports rose nearly 120 percent (Figure 2d). The deficit commonly represents a quarter or more of the GDP. An array of foreign loans and assistance, added to remittances from Belizeans living in the United States, bring in the foreign exchange to cover this trade deficit.[7] Also important in this regard have been increases in direct private investment flows. A drop in international aid or a major decline in any of the country's leading exports would seriously threaten the country's economic stability.

The country's small economic scale renders it ill-equipped to absorb even minor setbacks or downturns in the international market. Increased fuel costs or sinking sugar prices can have a disastrous impact on a $350 million economy. One asset of such a small economy is that even minor infusions of foreign economic aid or of other sources of foreign exchange (tourism or remittances) can stabilize the country's finances. Remittances account for at least $20 million annually.

The rapid growth of imports signaled an expanding economy, particularly with the increase in intermediate and capital goods imports (Figure 2e). But the country's increased import bill also illustrated several underlying weaknesses in the economy: Belize's small import-substitution manufacturing sector, its continuing need to import large amounts of food, and the heavy preference of consumers for imported goods. Historical patterns partly explain the country's import dependence. During the colonial era the government discouraged local agriculture while promoting imported items, particularly those from Britain.

The country's small size and low buying power have also discouraged the development of industries that depend on economies of scale.

Belize faces major challenges in the international market of the 1990s. External terms of trade for its major export commodities are expected to deteriorate through the mid-1990s.[8] Export expansion is

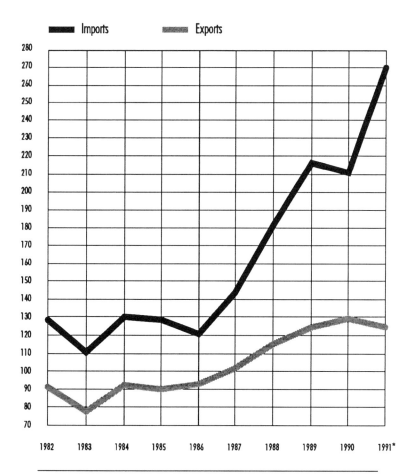

Figure 2d

Foreign Trade, 1982-1991

Millions of U.S. $.

SOURCE: IMF International Financial Statistics Yearbook 1989 and January 1992.
*Estimate.

also hampered by the sluggish economies of its two major trading partners, the United States and Britain.

The country's major exports depend on preferential access to the large industrial markets of the United States and Europe. With the U.S. market, the most important links are the sugar import quota program and the Caribbean Basin Initiative (CBI). The U.S. sugar program has enabled Belize to sell as much as a fifth of its sugar to the United States at prices considerably higher than those offered on the competitive world market. Because Belize is a CBI beneficiary, its agricultural exports have been exempt from U.S. import duties since 1984. Belizean producers, particularly citrus growers, were pleased when in 1990 Washington extended the CBI program indefinitely. However, U.S. trade liberalization initiatives, namely the proposed North American Free Trade Agreement (NAFTA) with Mexico and the Enterprise for the Americas Initiative (EAI), create new fears

Figure 2e
Leading Imports, 1991

Retained, not re-exported.

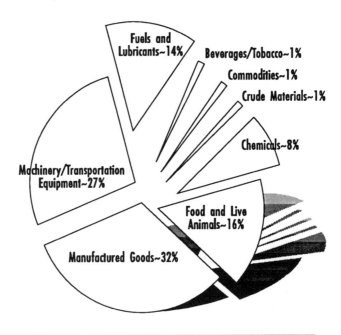

SOURCE: Office of Central Statistics, U.S. Embassy, Belize, February 1992.

that Washington will soon terminate all preferential trade programs in the name of free trade. Another major concern is that progress will be made in agricultural trade liberalization through the GATT (General Agreement on Tariffs and Trade) talks, thereby accelerating free trade in the agricultural sector.

In Europe, Belize benefits from the provisions of the Lomé Convention, under which some sixty third world countries, including those of the Commonwealth Caribbean, enjoy quotas for the low-tariff entry of certain agricultural goods. Belizean sugar and bananas, for example, enjoy preferential access to European markets. Plans for an expanded European Community raise concerns that the highly favorable trade provisions of the Lomé Convention may soon fade away. The Lomé agreement will next be negotiated in 1994, at which time its present beneficiaries will fight to keep current accords largely in place.

As a member of the Caribbean Community (Caricom), Belize also enjoys preferential trade rights in the Caribbean region. Being the largest citrus producer within Caricom, Belize can market its citrus concentrate in the region without fear of competition from non-Caricom producers. If free trade were to sweep through Latin America and break down this trade barrier, Belizean producers would no longer be able to count on a protected Caribbean market for its produce.

Because of its heavy dependence on preferential markets, Belize will be in a particularly vulnerable position if these quota and low-tariff programs are dismantled. Given its minimal economies of scale, relatively high labor costs, and low productivity, Belize cannot compete effectively in the free market. Lower cost producers throughout Latin America will quickly push aside Belizean exporters, while agricultural and manufactured goods from Guatemala, Mexico, and the United States will smother virtually all existing import-substitution production if free unconditional trade prevails.

"The inescapable conclusion arising from this world trend is that small countries such as Belize must strive for broad economic and trade cooperation, increased international competitiveness, level of productivity, and export capability," reasoned Economic Development Minister Said Musa.[9] Although Belize recognizes to a certain extent that free trade is inevitable, it is also committed to defending—for as long as possible—the secured and favored markets it has achieved for many of its exports.

Poverty and Wages

The United Nations Development Program ranks Belize among the most advanced nations in the region. The country's social indicators (including life expectancy, adult literacy, and average education) and its per capita GNP place Belize after Costa Rica and Panama but ahead of Nicaragua, El Salvador, Honduras, and Guatemala.[10] Per capita income for Belize in 1990 was approximately $1,600, with no income-distribution figures available.

Poverty is nonetheless widespread in Belize, although not to the desperate degree seen elsewhere in the region. Rural areas also suffer from less access to government services, and available educational and health services are of poorer quality than found in urban areas (see Health and Education). Eight percent of children under the age of one are malnourished as are 19 percent of those between one and 4 years, with the highest incidences of malnutrition found in the southern districts of Stann Creek and Toledo.

The rapid growth of the informal sector in the 1980s reflected the lack of decent-paying jobs available in the formal economy. This was readily apparent in the sharp increase in street vendors and house-to-house retailers.[11]

In an attempt to ensure that economic growth is more broadly shared, the government established a Minimum Wage Council as the first step toward raising the minimum wage, which stood at $1.25 an hour in early 1992. Proposals to increase the minimum wage to as much as $2.25 faced strong opposition by the Chamber of Commerce and other business groups. The chamber argued that a low inflation rate (3-4 percent annually between 1986 and 1991) made an increase in the minimum wage unnecessary. Besides swelling inflation, higher wages would make it more difficult for Belize to compete in the shrinking export market. The chamber was also concerned that higher wages would entail increased employer contributions to Social Security.

Industry and Infrastructure

Most of the manufactured goods consumed by Belizeans are imported or bought directly in the Mexican border city of Chetumal. Representing only 10 percent of the GDP, the manufacturing sector is composed mostly of agroindustries such as flour milling, citrus-concentrate extraction, and feed production. There is also a small import-substitution industrial sector (benefiting from high protective tariffs) that produces beer, soft drinks, cigarettes, furniture, and building materials for the local market. Rounding out the industrial sector are several garment-assembly plants that produce almost exclusively for the U.S. market, mostly on a contract basis. The most prominent of these is Williamson Industries, which has been in Belize for two decades and employs some 600 workers at its plant outside Belize City.

Smaller operations include a few Korean- and Chinese-owned plants that produce garments for Sears and K-Mart in the United States.

Low labor productivity and high wage levels (relative to neighboring countries) dim the prospects for a booming export-oriented manufacturing sector in Belize. Concessions offered by other Central American countries, the high cost of electricity, and the small Belizean labor force also limit the future for export manufacturing. Belize does hope, however, to attract more assembly industries to its San Andres Export-Processing Zone (EPZ) on the Mexican border, where industries are able to take advantage of less-expensive Mexican electricity.

According to a 1984 World Bank report on Belize, "Geological evidence indicates a good possibility that Belize has significant deposits of oil and gas, both onshore and offshore." Current exploration for oil and gas is taking place in northwestern Belize, which is part of the Petén basin where geological formations are equivalent to those of the Reforma and Chiapas oil and gas fields in Mexico.[12]

Economic development in Belize has been constrained by the country's poor infrastructure, particularly its transportation system. The lack of cross-country roads was not a problem for the timber industry—which formed the economic backbone of Belize until the 1950s—since logs were floated down river to the seaports. But as an agriculture sector developed, led by the sugar cane industry, a road system became essential to economic progress.

The Northern Highway, running from the Mexican border to Belize City, was the country's first paved artery. The next effort was the Western Highway in 1948, which transverses the country from Belize City to Benque Viejo on the western border with Guatemala. Linking prior and present capitals, the stretch from Belize City to Belmopan is the best maintained in the country. The Hummingbird Highway, heading southeast from Belmopan to Dangriga (35 miles by sea from Belize City), still leaves a lot to be desired but is undergoing major renovation. The Southern Highway, which descends from outside Dangriga to Punta Gorda at Belize's southern tip, remains unpaved, although the portion used by the banana industry is being widened and improved.

Buoyed by foreign assistance (mainly in the form of concessional loans), the government mounted an extensive infrastructure-expansion program in the late 1980s which continues today. External money covered more than 60 percent of public-sector capital investment in the 1986-90 period. Roads, ports, and airports have been designed to boost agroexport agriculture and tourism—the country's main sources of foreign exchange. Meanwhile, social services remain underfunded.

Infrastructure activity is booming in Belize; the construction industry is the country's fastest-growing sector. Roads are being upgraded and old single-lane wooden bridges are being replaced with financial assistance mainly from the United States and Europe. The Caribbean Development Bank and Britain jointly sponsored the expansion of the Philip Goldson International Airport, finished in 1990. International capital also financed a new deepwater port at Big Creek, chiefly to facilitate the export of bananas and citrus. Rural electrification made great strides in the 1980s with support from the World Bank. To reduce its reliance on imported oil and decrease the cost of electricity, a major hydroelectric plant is planned along a remote stretch of the Macal River in the Cayo district.

Telephone service has expanded rapidly, placing Belize Telecommunications, a joint public-private venture, among the country's most profitable companies. Pay telephones are now found even in remote locations. A notable advance was the completion of a modern water and sewerage system in Belize City, sponsored by the Canadian International Development Agency. Also in Belize City new market and bridge construction is under way, while a new national stadium and hospital complex are in the planning stage.

Sun, Sea, and Ecotourism

In the 1960s some 11,000 foreigners visited Belize each year. That figure jumped to 30,000 ten years later, rising to 64,000 by 1980 and reaching 190,000 in 1990, with an average annual growth rate of 15-20 percent in the late 1980s. The tourism industry is booming in Belize, helped in part by the government's new promotional campaign inviting tourists to "Belize—The Adventure Coast, Undiscovered and Unspoiled." Tourism now ranks second to sugar production as a source of foreign exchange. The main tourist attraction is the country's spectacular barrier reef and the nearby small islands called cayes. The some 600 archeological sites and the frontier quality of the Belizean environment are also tourist draws. Counting on the foreign-exchange value of what is called "ecotourism," the government has shifted more attention to environmental conservation, as best illustrated in its declaration of new protected areas.

The tourism industry was birthed on Ambergris Caye, the country's largest and most northerly island. Small investors in San Pedro (the island's population center), mainly from the United States, began privately promoting Belize as a fishing, diving, and snorkeling paradise. With no encouragement or even much interest from the national government, San Pedro hoteliers single-handedly put Belize on the map of international tourism.

According to a United Nations' report in the 1960s, the PUP "virtually frowned on the industry and from all accounts did its utmost to discourage its development."[13] In contrast, the UDP, committed to deregulation and uncontrolled foreign investment, threw the doors of the country open to the tourism industry when it became the ruling party in 1985, considering it a bountiful source of foreign exchange. Tourism became the country's second development priority, rising from seventh place. Upon returning to office, the PUP dropped its previous ambivalence about tourism and has vigorously promoted the industry while placing an increased emphasis on ecotourism.

In Belize, as elsewhere, the ecotourist came before ecotourism. Searching for natural and culturally distinct environments, the conservation-minded ecotourist traveled to Belize, attracted more by the country's laid-back atmosphere and its pristine natural environment than by simple "sun and fun" tourism. Snorkeling and diving on the reef were only one part of the attraction of ecotourists to Belize. The country also had vast tracts of rainforest, abundant flora and fauna, and dozens of Mayan ruins. Belize offered a great escape from the cold and stress of the North but without the usual tourism hype and gloss. Instead of staying in carpeted luxury hotels, ecotourists preferred family-run hotels and restaurants.

The early ecotourists sparked a new consciousness in the tourism industry that there were dollars to be made in catering to this new breed of international visitors. Belize has enthusiastically embraced this windfall by hosting international ecotourism conferences, opening new forest reserves, and welcoming the participation of such foreign organizations as the Audubon Society, Conservation International, and World Wildlife Fund in conservation and development planning (see Environment).

The country's former disinclination to promote tourism was in part a reaction to the colonial experience. The PUP was wary of more foreign influence at the very time it was seeking independence and searching for a national identity. Traditional international tourism was also regarded as an ineffective basis for economic development, creating little spin-off employment in the local economy since a large part of its inputs are imported. With few domestic industries, an almost nonexistent arts and crafts tradition, and with most of its investment in foreign hands, the tourism industry is particularly plagued by the lack of multiplier effects. Another longstanding concern has been that tourism would mainly benefit foreign investors, while local Belizeans would be burdened by inflated land and consumer prices. More recently, government planners and environmentalists have expressed the fear that tourism, even ecotourism, is leaving its own trail of environmental problems.

Nowhere are the dangers of tourism so evident as in San Pedro. Although the population is economically better off than it was three decades ago, the tourism industry is dominated by foreigners. With expatriates amounting to half the population, land prices have soared to absurd heights. There are still remnants of family-based services, but the bulk of the business is controlled by U.S. investors. The residents of San Pedro have for the most part watched their piece of Caribbean paradise slip out of their hands. "They are little more than slaves now, working for outsiders," grumbled a former fisherman turned hotelier who lives on the neighboring Caye Caulker. In contrast to the more developed island, tourism remains a family business in Caye Caulker, with all sea-front property remaining in local hands. Joy Grant, director of Program for Belize, criticizes the "runaway development" in San Pedro, saying that such haphazard tourism development of the cayes has led to contamination of the water, a sewage disposal crisis, loss of mangrove habitats, and a reduction of fish stock on the reef.[14]

The number of hotels in Belize soared from 61 in 1974 to more than 225 by 1992. The early 1990s saw the opening or expansion of major luxury hotels in Belize City, including the new Ramada Royal Reef Hotel and Marina. But Belize stands in no danger of becoming another Cancun. The first-class hotels in Belize City are often nearly empty, and only one-fourth of the country's hotels are regarded as acceptable by the Caribbean Tourism Research and Development Center.[15] Foreign investors control most of the country's best hotels and lodges, but the majority of hotels and guest houses are still locally owned and operated.

Closely related to the ecotourism boom is the regional La Ruta Maya or El Mundo Maya tourism development project involving Mexico, Guatemala, and Belize, and to a lesser extent Honduras and El Salvador. Sponsored mainly by private interests, El Mundo Maya is a marketing concept promoting the archeological, environmental, and cultural attractions in the Middle America region. The Mundo Maya promoters hope to facilitate intercountry travel in the region with improved road networks and rapid customs processing, and they are promoting the creation of binational and trinational parks and reserves in the region. Belize has been tentatively selected as the site for the headquarters of El Mundo Maya.

Aside from the absence of quality hotels, Belize also lacks the transportation infrastructure to handle the increase in tourists that El Mundo Maya campaign is expected to bring to the region. An expanded airport terminal outside Belize City, a new airstrip in Caye Caulker, and others planned for San Pedro, Placentia, Punta Gorda, and San Ignacio will help the tourism industry. New road projects will facilitate the extension of tourism to previously inaccessible regions while at the same time boosting rural development. But with this infrastructure expansion Belize will also be losing some of the rustic, undeveloped qualities that make it so attractive to a certain set of visitors.

Even before it gets off the ground, El Mundo Maya has met with some criticism by the local Maya population for its lack of involvement of Mayas in the conception and development of the project. Pedro Cucul, a Maya spokesperson, advised a tourism conference held in Belize that "anything that affects the culture of the Maya should be discussed with them." Similarly, Sylvia Flores, mayor of Dangriga, warned that "we must be sensitized to the possible negative effects" of tourism, and we must examine "what great impact the coming of people from other lands has had on our culture."[16]

The Drug Business—Marijuana to Crack

Belize has never been and probably never will be high on the charts of Latin America's sugar or citrus exporters. But it briefly rose to the upper ranks of Latin American drug exporters to the United States. In the early 1980s the U.S. Drug Enforcement Administration (DEA) listed Belize as the fourth-largest source of U.S. marijuana imports. To combat the drug menace, Washington obliged the Belizean government to undertake an aerial spraying program, providing the country's police with the airplanes and chemicals (largely paraquat) needed for the eradication campaign. The DEA eradication program proved successful in lowering Belize's marijuana exports, slashing the annual exports of "Belize Breeze" from 200 tons in the mid-1980s to 50 tons by the end of the decade. Belize is now considered a "marginal producer."[17] Rising prices and an expanding market in more traditional agroexports in the late 1980s also contributed to the decline in marijuana cultivation. The campaign, while successful in its objective, was not well received by the farming community, which complained that the aerial spraying destroyed legitimate crops as well as the illegal one.

In the 1980s the openness of the marijuana drug culture in Belize was reined in by the DEA's antinarcotics operations and by new civic efforts to combat individual drug use led by the Parents' Resource Institute for Drug Eradication (PRIDE). The "Say No" educational campaign has made an impact, and has been extended to such legal drugs as alcohol and valium. Alcoholism is a major social problem in Belize, where one can still see crude signboards promoting liquor, telling Belizeans that "It's Fun to Drink."

The hole in the international market left by Belize's decreased marijuana cultivation was filled, however, by increased production in Guatemala. But beginning in 1989, Belize became a major transshipment point for South American cocaine. According to the U.S. Bureau on International Narcotics, Belize has become "an important and vulnerable transit point for cocaine moving to the north along the Central American isthmus."

The transshipment business—no cocaine is produced in Belize—has fueled an insidious illegal economy that involves all levels of society—from the police and politicians who are on the take to the "base boys" in Belize City who have switched from ganja to deadly crack. So apparent is the drug money, especially in border towns, that some local observers consider drugs to be the top business in Belize. The decline in marijuana use and the rapid proliferation of crack habits has been accompanied by a rise in street crime and gang violence. Both the police and the military have mounted major antinarcotics campaigns that round up street hustlers and those who frequent crack houses, but they never seem to catch the big fish. The street wisdom is that if they ever went after the large dealers and smugglers there would be hell to pay for the politicians.

U.S. military assistance to Belize is authorized largely because it backs counternarcotics operations. According to the U.S. Department of Defense, Belizean narcotraffickers work closely with Guatemalan guerrillas—a relationship that it calls "potentially destabilizing."[18] Washington offers no evidence documenting this cooperation, though cases of collaboration between drug traffickers and the security forces of both Guatemala and Belize frequently come to light.

The Agricultural Economy

The Belize national anthem exhorts Belizeans: "Arise, ye sons of the Baymen's clan. . . . No longer shall we be hewers of wood." Unlike the other British colonies in the Caribbean, Belize does not have a history of large agroexport plantations operated with slave labor. The slaves of Belize did not cut cane; instead, they cut down logwood for export to Europe. When the logwood market contracted, the forestry industry turned to mahogany and other fine woods. *Chicle* (a gum extracted from the sapodilla tree) was another mainstay of the colony's forestry industry.

No longer, however, are Belizeans major hewers of wood. Forestry lost its leading place in the Belizean economy in the 1960s and by the 1990s accounted for less than 3 percent of export income—mainly in the form of sawn wood rather than finished wood products. The lack of new penetration roads and the failure of the loggers to reforest contributed to the decline of this once-thriving industry. Although slight in terms of the total economy, the amount of board feet of lumber exported in the 1980s actually increased by two-thirds.

Agricultural exports provide 65-70 percent of the country's foreign exchange. Unprocessed agricultural commodities have long been the foundation of the Belizean economy, and a highly skewed structure of land ownership characterizes the agricultural sector. The agricultural economy was first dominated by logwood, then mahogany, and then sugar. In the 1970s sugar became the undisputed king in Belize, accounting for 60 percent of the country's export income. Although sugar still reigns supreme, other commodities—citrus, bananas, seafood, and cacao—constitute a slightly more diversified export offering. With the exception of assembled garments, all leading exports come from the agricultural sector.

Belize's export offering of sugar, citrus, bananas, and cacao—sometimes called a breakfast economy—is produced by low-paid labor and involves little value-added processing (Figure 2f). Efficiency in the production of these agroexports is considerably below international levels, leading to high production costs and reduced comparative advantage on the world market. However, because of Belize's preferential trade relationships with major consuming nations, this relative inefficiency is not currently a major obstacle in marketing. Although Belize does produce most of its basic staples except wheat, during the 1980s corn production stagnated and rice production dropped significantly. The country has, however, become self-sufficient in poultry, eggs, finished animal feed (a result of Mennonite church efforts), and milk. The vegetable market is characterized by alternating gluts and scarcity as a result of seasonal production trends.

Sugar—The Backbone of Export Agriculture

Sugar cane has been cultivated in Belize since the 17th century but it was not until the 1960s that cane products (sugar and molasses) became a major player in the economy. Two sugar factories owned and operated by the British sugar giant Tate & Lyle quickly established sugar as the country's economic leader in the 1960s. Sugar and molasses production boomed in the 1970s. Low world prices pushed the industry into a slump in the early 1980s, with export income dropping by more than half between 1980 and 1985. The 1985 decision by Tate & Lyle to close the Libertad processing plant and divest 90 percent of its holding in the Tower Hill plant shocked the industry, but with government assistance and improved sugar prices the sugar industry gradually restructured and recovered. The revived Libertad plant produces molasses as a feedstock for ethanol

Figure 2f

Export Value of Agricultural Commodities, 1980-1990

Thousands of U.S. $.

	1980	1990
Sugar	47,700	42,700
Citrus concentrate		
Grapefruit	2,100	4,800
Orange	3,900	16,800
Bananas	3,500	9,800
Fish products	3,700	9,000
Cacao	12	450

SOURCE: Central Statistical Office (Belmopan).

manufacture in Jamaica by the Jamaican state oil company Petro-jam, and the Tower Hill plant is now owned by Belize Sugar Industries (BSI), a local company that has a marketing agreement with Tate & Lyle.

Some 59,000 acres in the Corozal and Orange Walk districts are cultivated by more than 5,000 sugar cane farmers, who employ thousands of seasonal workers during the harvest. Ninety-three percent of production is destined for the export market. By 1990 production had again passed the 100,000 long ton mark, just below the 1980 peak. Sugar remains the predominant agroexport, typically accounting for 30-40 percent of the country's export income—more than citrus and bananas combined.

Although the sugar cane industry has recuperated from its slump, it still suffers from inefficient transport and processing facilities as well as overcapitalization by many growers (too much equipment for the land they cultivate). More worrisome for the future of the industry, however, is its continued dependence on preferential U.S., Canadian, and European markets. Under the U.S. sugar import quotas system, Belize enjoys a 1.1 percent quota of U.S. sugar imports, with the quantity and price changing each year according to the size of the U.S. shortfall. Between 1989 and 1991 the U.S. sugar quota for Belize was cut in half, dropping from 29,000 metric tons to 14,500 metric tons. In contrast, the sugar protocol of the European Community sets a fixed quantity of sugar that can be imported preferentially. Prices received in these two preferential markets are twice as high as those on the world market. About 35 percent of Belize's sugar is sold on the world market, where prices undergo extreme fluctuation and are often only marginally above production costs.

If Belize's preferential access is closed, the sugar industry might collapse. It is likely that the U.S. sugar import program will be eliminated in the 1990s, and although the sugar protocol with the EC may continue, guaranteed prices will likely drop sharply. With lower efficiency and higher production costs, Belize would have a difficult time competing on the world market with other major sugar producers. Also looming as a threat to the sugar industry is the possible resumption of Cuba's place as a major sugar exporter to the United States. Given this gloomy future, crop diversification and the downsizing of sugar production in northern Belize is necessary for the continued economic health of the Corozal and Orange Walk districts.[19]

Citrus

The citrus industry is the country's second most important agricultural activity. A small planting of grapefruit in 1913 followed by serious commercial production of citrus in 1924 (with investments by a British expatriate) marked the beginning of the industry in Belize.[20] Today, orange and grapefruit groves—or "walks" as they are called in Belize—parallel the Hummingbird Highway as it winds through Stann Creek Valley and along the Maya Mountains. Although citrus is also cultivated in Cayo, the industry is centered in the Southeast where the country's two citrus processing plants are located. The two plants, Belize Food Products and the Citrus Company of Belize, export orange and grapefruit concentrate.

The 1984 Caribbean Basin Initiative, which eliminated the 30 percent import duty on most agricultural products, galvanized Belize's citrus industry. Between 1980 and 1990 the value of citrus exports, mostly orange juice, more than tripled. By 1990 more than 40,000 acres were under citrus cultivation. Ninety-six percent of the country's citrus crop is exported as frozen juice concentrate to the United States, the Caricom market, and Europe.

The upswing in the citrus industry has encouraged many small growers with access to government credit and technical assistance to switch from corn and rice farming to citrus cultivation.[21] More than four hundred growers supply the citrus plants, with 30 percent of production controlled by large landowners. Tensions and conflicts over pricing and technical assistance pit small growers against large growers and processing plants, as is true in the sugar industry. In the mid-1970s, independent growers held back production in a successful protest to demand higher prices from the processing plants.

Although prices have improved substantially, the control exercised by the two processing plants and the large growers remains a continuing source of conflict in the industry. This imbalance is reflected in the disproportionate power of the relatively few large growers in the Citrus Growers Association. Even the smallest scale farmer on the CGA managing committee, who is sometimes identified as the "small man's representative," owns substantially more land than most Stann Creek citrus farmers.[22]

At the base of the industry are the thousands of seasonal workers who pick the oranges. Paid by the box, these workers are mostly Spanish-speaking migrants, many of whom are undocumented. Citing a shortage of labor during the harvest season (October through March), the large growers request work permits to hire temporary laborers, mainly from Guatemala and El Salvador.[23] These workers, who live in squalid conditions near the processing factories and corporate estates, are brutally exploited by the citrus growers. Despite the government's involvement in granting work permits for many of these farm laborers, growers routinely violate the country's labor laws and threaten to tear up the permits if the workers complain about ill treatment or about being underpaid.

Besides their vulnerability as undocumented or permit workers, the citrus pickers are also victims of creole and Garifuna anti-Spanish racism as well as a labor hierarchy that relegates them to the hardest and lowest-paid work. The unions that represent citrus workers are controlled by the creoles and Garifunas who work at much-higher-paying jobs in transport and in the factories.[24]

At a time when citrus production appears on the verge of a major expansion, liberalization of world trading patterns and the formation of new regional trading blocks cast a shadow over the industry. Washington's free trade initiatives are the main concern of Belize's citrus industry. If Belizean producers are forced to compete on equal terms with Mexican and Brazilian growers, the country's citrus industry might collapse. Another concern is the possibility that Caricom might be opened to non-English-speaking countries in the region, thereby undermining Belize's position as the main supplier of citrus concentrate to Trinidad and Barbados.

Adding to these uncertain market prospects are the industry's internal problems, including outdated technology, marketing deficiencies, and inefficient productivity.[25] Another concern is the encouragement the citrus boom gives growers to clear forests and expand onto unsuitable soils.

Bananas and Seafood

The banana industry dates back to 1880 when U.S. and British investors created banana enclaves in the South. Banana exports helped open a trade route between New Orleans and British Honduras.[26] Banana production peaked in 1917, after which the Panama disease struck the plantations and dampened production until 1923. In the 1930s the banana industry was hit by Stikatoka, or leaf spot disease, which again decimated production. Disease and hurricanes have repeatedly cut short the country's potential as a major banana exporter.

In 1971 the government through the Banana Control Board and United Brands through its marketing subsidiary Fyffes Group launched an expansion of the banana industry in southern Stann Creek and Toledo, introducing disease-resistant trees. The government had the dual objective of increasing export income and reducing unemployment in this depressed rural area. In the early 1980s banana production first stagnated, then soared by the end of the decade. Between 1980 and 1990 banana export income tripled.

Like so many other things in Belize, even the good news about increased banana exports became a local political football. The UDP government claimed that increased exports were the direct result of privatization of investments by the Banana Control Board in 1986. In response, the PUP asserted that its own earlier direct support of banana production—with government investments in roads, electricity, water, housing, and corporate offices—provided the necessary foundation for the industry's current takeoff.

Banana production in Belize is inefficient when compared with production levels achieved by growers in Honduras and Costa Rica. Small farmers have difficulty raising enough working capital to maintain efficient production. Like sugar and citrus, bananas are exported under the preferential terms of the Lomé Convention, so the planned creation of a single European market might adversely impact the banana industry in Belize. If its secured access to the European market is blocked, then Belizean producers will have to compete directly against the lower cost, more efficient producers of the region. Belize produces about 11 tons per acre, while Costa Rica and Honduras each produce more than 14 tons per acre. Belize's bananas are produced for export to Britain under contract with Fyffes Group, which was one of the major sources of financing for the deep-water port at Big Creek. The ability to ship bananas directly from Belize rather than transshipping them on barges to Honduras has boosted the prospects for the banana industry, which has plenty of room for expansion in undeveloped southern Belize.

In the 1980-90 period the export value of seafood products (mainly conch, lobster, and shrimp) more than doubled, but production remained constant. Although benefiting from higher export prices, the fishing cooperatives that dominate the industry are facing a depletion of the country's marine life. Despite the increased numbers of fishermen, the catches of conch and lobster actually declined in the 1980s. Shrimp trawling resulted in a doubling of production in the 1986-90 period. But there is growing concern that like conch and lobster fishing, the shrimp industry may also be operating at or beyond the level of maximum sustainable yield. Besides foreign demand for the country's marine products, the fishing industry has enjoyed increased demand by the local tourism industry. One result is that many fishermen sell illegal catches (such as young lobsters) to tourist restaurants on the cayes.

Nontraditional Agroexports

Crop diversification has had only limited success in Belize. The major success has been cacao production by Hummingbird Hershey, a subsidiary of the Hershey Foods Corporation, which began producing commercially in 1977. As part of its search for greater productivity and increased flavor, Hershey operates its own small plantation in Belize and also buys 15 percent of its cacao from small growers. Between 1980 and 1990 the value of Belize's cacao exports increased almost 40-fold.

The Caribbean Basin Initiative opened up the U.S. market to nontraditional agroexports from Belize, while the U.S. Agency for International Development (AID) provided the funds to boost production of such exports as cacao, spices, and mangoes. The AID-funded Belize Agri-Business Company (BABCO) has experimented with a wide range of winter vegetables and fruit, hoping to alleviate the dependency of northern farmers on sugar cane. But sugar cane growers and *milperos* (slash-and-burn farmers) in other parts of the country have proved reluctant to switch from sugar cane and basic grains to nontraditional exports without guaranteed markets. Another problem has been the failure of Belize to attract foreign investment in nontraditional agroexport production. In mid-1987 the failure of the U.S.-owned Caribe Farm Industries seriously deflated hopes for rising exports of winter vegetables and fruit to the United States.

There is, however, still hope that papaya production will take hold in northern Belize as a partial alternative to cane cropping. A boost in nontraditional fruit production, especially mango exports, is expected in southern Belize with the 1990 acquisition by Fyffes Group of a European company specializing in exotic tropical fruits and by the production of Belize Gold mangoes by the Tropical Produce Company. One local success story is the export of Tennessee Red peanuts to the Caricom market by the Belize Federation of Agricultural Cooperatives and a private firm called Friendly Foods. Melinda's carrot-and-chile-based hot sauce, another small agroexport, has become a hit in the United States.

Staple Crops

As a country that imports nearly a quarter of what it eats and drinks, there is much room for improvement in the food production system. Actually Belize has made considerable headway in basic foods production for the local market in the last three decades. The country has achieved nominal self-sufficiency in bean, corn, and (until recently) rice production. Belize regularly exports dry red kidney beans, beyond those consumed in Belize, and production of these beans tripled in the 1980s. Official figures, however, do not accurately reflect the degree of food self-sufficiency in Belize because widespread contraband importation of cheaper basic foodstuffs from neighboring countries is not reported.

Most farmers in Belize work small plots. Larger scale operations include those of the Mennonite communities and a handful of large landholders (with over 200 hectares), who own as much as 60 percent of the country's productive agricultural land.[27] Some home-grown successes have been achieved. For example, milk production has increased dramatically, rising from just 600,000 pounds of milk in 1980 to 2,700,000 by 1990, making Belize self-sufficient in that commodity.

After rising, albeit at an erratic pace, corn production leveled off in the 1980s. In 1990 the country produced 41 million pounds of corn on 24,000 acres—approximately the same amount as in 1980. Slash-and-burn *milpa* farming is gradually declining in Belize while machine cultivation, almost exclusively by Mennonites, has become steadily more important. With increased small-farm efficiency, surplus corn could be an exportable item in the future. But relatively high production costs in Belize make identifying a profitable foreign market difficult.

Belize is no longer self-sufficient in rice largely as a result of the demise of Big Falls Ranch, the country's major source of mechanized rice production. Rice production declined from a high of 24 million pounds in 1981 to 10 million pounds by 1990. Per capita consumption of rice, the key staple in the traditional Belizean diet, is 87 pounds a year. Rice production in Belize is inefficient, and the country could quadruple production levels if improved varieties and more efficient methods of cultivation were utilized.[28]

Fresh vegetables do not have a prominent place in the Belizean diet and are available only seasonally on a "feast or famine" basis. Vegetables are usually planted commercially only during the cooler months from November to February, and home gardens are rare. A Livestock Development Project sponsored by AID aims to increase beef and pork production in Belize, which though rising still falls short of local demand. Ranches of more than 50 acres raise about two-thirds of the nation's livestock and are located mainly in the Belize River Valley.[29]

Most of the country's food imports are items that are not produced in Belize. Condensed milk, cheese, and powdered milk are imported, as is all the country's wheat and most of its potatoes, onions, lard, margarine, and beverage flavoring. The country's major meat imports are preserved or prepared meat products, such as corned beef, ham, and sausages.

The Mennonites of Spanish Lookout, Blue Creek, and Shipyard produce the bulk of the eggs and poultry consumed in Belize. Their well-organized and vertically integrated production systems result in cheaper eggs and poultry than those raised by others who have attempted to enter this profitable market. One major advantage is their ability to supply their businesses with all the animal feed they need.

Having expanded three-fold in the 1980s, the poultry industry has been able to meet the country's demand for chicken meat.

Although the government has a policy of food self-reliance, there is little in the way of technical or financial assistance available for small farmers producing for the internal market. Instead, farmers producing for export enjoy favored access to credit and technical assistance. Belize does have a Marketing Board, which was established to assist small farmers with storage and marketing but is now largely nonfunctional. Earlier government programs to promote the small-farm economy have been mostly abandoned for financial and administrative reasons. Setting high prices for basic grains did prove successful in promoting increased production, but in 1980 the government discovered that it could buy lower-priced grains on the international market and realized that it was incurring severe losses when exporting grain surpluses.

At the insistence of the IMF and AID, Belize curtailed its price subsidies and its programs to assist small farmers with storage and marketing. The early dreams of transforming Belize into a major grains producer—symbolized by the empty grain silos constructed in Belmopan—have since faded. What remains is a half-hearted commitment to food self-sufficiency, while inadequate storage facilities and marketing infrastructure continue to handicap rural development in Belize.[30]

The country's small *milpa* farmers (mostly Indian and *mestizo*) have not been given a favored place in Belize's agricultural development program. There are some 6,000 subsistence or sub-subsistence *milperos* growing mainly corn and beans in roadless areas and on mountain slopes. These small growers have little access to credit or technical assistance. Slightly above this level is a group of small farmers (mainly *mestizo*) who produce basic grains for national consumption. The slash-and-burn method practiced by these farmers has already deforested—and threatens to erode—the hilly land they farm.

3

Society and Ethnicity

© Debra Preusch

A Multi-ethnic, Multilingual Society

Belize is an extraordinarily diverse society—culturally, ethnically, and linguistically. Only the rare Belizean can claim to be a descendant of the native Amerindian population. The original inhabitants were either killed or driven out of the territory by the Spanish and the British or had fallen victim to epidemic diseases by the time British Honduras was declared a colony in 1862.

The origin of one prominent ethnic group, the creoles, comes from the mating of early British settlers with African slaves brought from Jamaica to labor in the logging camps from 1720 to the early 1800s. All later racial combinations of Europeans or North Americans with the local population also form part of the creole group. Creoles, whose skin color ranges from fair to very dark, constituted about 30 percent of the population in 1991, and are geographically concentrated in the Belize district, where two-thirds of them live. Belize City is more than 50 percent creole. Creoles are also found living along the country's main highways and rivers as well as in rural villages like Monkey River, Bermuda Landing, and Burrell Boom.

More than 40 percent of the people are *mestizos*, whose first language is Spanish. For the most part, *mestizos* are not descendants of early Spanish colonists but of the thousands of mixed-blood Mexicans and Yucatec Mayas who fled from the Yucatán in the mid-1800s to escape the bloodletting of the War of the Castes. Doubling the territory's population, these immigrants settled in the northern lowlands, bringing with them a strong agricultural tradition. Because of the continuing flow of refugees, economically displaced immigrants, and seasonal farmworkers into Belize from Guatemala, El Salvador, and Honduras, the *mestizo* population is the most rapidly rising ethnic grouping and already constitutes the largest segment of this polyglot society (see Immigration and Emigration). *Mestizos* are concentrated along the New River corridor running from Corozal to Orange Walk Town, in the towns of Benque Viejo and San Ignacio, in west-central

Belize, and in recent strip settlements along the Hummingbird Highway in the middle of the citrus district.

Over three-fourths of the people of Orange Walk and Corozal districts speak Spanish as their first language. With the influx of Central American refugees and continual creole emigration, the Spanish-speaking population is becoming increasingly dominant in many parts of Belize, even in Belize City. A new national holiday, Pan American Day, replaces Columbus Day and celebrates the Latin heritage. Census figures released in mid-1992 revealed that *mestizos* are now the largest single ethnic group in Belizean society.

In 1991 the Garifuna community, which speaks its own language in addition to English and which has its own culture, formed 6.6 percent of the population. As with all other ethnic groups, except *mestizos*, the Garifuna proportion of the total population has decreased since 1980. Yet over half of Stann Creek district is Garifuna. Aside from the telltale evidence of their surnames, language, and geographical location, it is difficult even for most Belizeans to distinguish Garifunas from creoles. Nonetheless, there exists continuing racial animosity between the two groups of Afro-Belizeans. In an effort to promote understanding and solidarity, a unified Afro-Belizean group was founded in Belize City in early 1991.

There are three Amerindian groups in Belize: the Yucatec in the northern districts, who have largely merged with the *mestizo* population, and the Mopan and Kekchí, who emigrated from Guatemala and who are concentrated in the Toledo district with about 7,000 in each grouping. After slavery was abolished in 1838 and especially in the 1860s the British brought indentured servants from China and India to Belize. Distinct communities of East Indians remain although they no longer speak Hindi, and the early Chinese population of Belize has been supplemented in recent years by a new flow of Chinese immigrants. Because of their ownership of many shops and restaurants, the some 1,200 Chinese residents have gained a prominent place in Belizean society. For some Chinese families, Belize is just a stepping stone to the United States. Adding to the potpourri are a few families of Lebanese descent who have distinguished themselves in politics and commerce.

Although English remains the language of business and politics, Spanish is becoming more widely spoken as the *mestizo* and Maya populations increase. The Garifuna and several Mayan communities speak their own languages, and a German-Dutch dialect is spoken by the Mennonites in Cayo and Orange Walk.[1] Creole is also being used more as a common language, although there are now both English and Spanish varieties of creole dialects.

The heterogeneous character of Belize is somewhat offset by the different geographical concentrations of each ethnic group. With the exception of the Mennonites, who marry exclusively within their small community of 6,000, there is a continuing mixture of all ethnic groups, which serves to ease racial tensions and create an overall Belizean national identity. Nonetheless, racial stereotyping and tensions do exist, albeit at a nonviolent level, and can be readily observed whenever Belizeans come together, whether it be on the Belize City-Cayo bus or in national politics.

Creole-*mestizo* tension is the principal manifestation of racial conflict. Recent immigrants from Central America have brought their anti-black prejudices with them, while creoles see these "aliens" or "Spanish" as a threat to their traditional political and numerical domination of Belizean society. They fear that the ongoing "latinization" of Belize is displacing what is commonly referred to as the "true Belizean." This sentiment was clearly expressed in an editorial column of the *Belize Review*. Arguing that the country needs to remain "predominantly black," the Belize City monthly stated, "There is no doubt that a great deal of the quality of life in Belize is due to the fact that it has a 'black' or African-based majority. . . . There is also no doubt that if any of the other groups ascended to majority status—increased latinization, for example—the character of Belize would change dramatically. . . . Belize today has absolutely no way to protect herself against a heavy influx of immigrants."[2]

Racial divisions certainly exist in Belize, but are manifested more in racial stereotyping than in direct competition or overt strife. The cultural and economic differences between the races are at least partly due to colonial "divide and rule" policies that assigned ethnic groups different roles in society. While racial prejudice is common, it is softened by a "live and let live" atmosphere that recognizes the special contributions of each ethnic group.[3]

Mennonites

The Mennonites in Belize trace their lineage back to villages in the Swiss Alps. They are members of a Protestant sect that migrated first to northern Germany and southern Russia, to Pennsylvania in the late 1700s, and to Canada a century later. Following World War I, some settled in Mexico in their persistent search for freedom of religion and freedom from state interference. The Mennonites in Belize began arriving in 1958, mostly from Manitoba, Canada, and Chihuahua, Mexico.[4]

They own large blocks of land (about 145,000 acres in total) and insist on control of their own schools and financial institutions, complete separation of church and state, and exemption from military service. Their innovations in agricultural production and marketing have been felt throughout the country. Their six main communities are Blue Creek, Shipyard, Little Belize, Progreso, Spanish Outlook, and Barton Creek in northern and northwestern Belize. Immediately recognizable—the men in dark trousers and cheap straw hats, the women in long dresses and bonnets, and the children with their freckled faces—the Mennonites have turned sections of rural Belize into neat and highly productive farmland and dairies, resembling parts of Minnesota or Pennsylvania.

The Mennonite community is divided into religiously progressive and conservative wings, with the progressives believing that the church should involve itself in the world while the more traditional contend that the modern world contaminates their pure faith. The Mennonite conservatives—clustered mostly in Shipyard, Little Belize, and Barton Creek—still refrain from using modern farm equipment, retain Low German as their primary language, and can be seen driving into rural villages in their horse-drawn buggies. In contrast, members of the modernizing tendency use telephones and listen to stereo music. Unlike their fundamentalist brethren who do no proselytizing, the progressives have sponsored missionary churches in Belize, including ones that specifically reach out to the Garifuna and Mayan communities. In Blue Creek, there is also an Evangelical Mennonite Mission Church, founded by members alienated from the Old Colony Church.[5]

Whether traditional or progressive, the Mennonites are widely respected in Belize for being hard-working, community-minded, and inventive. All Belizeans have benefited from their many contributions to the agricultural economy. Their poultry business, Quality Poultry Products, markets inexpensive, locally produced eggs and chicken meat throughout the country. In addition to enabling chicken to become the national dish, Mennonites craft elegant, sturdy wooden furniture that graces many Belizean homes.

Creoles

Belizean creoles are, for the most part, the descendants of slaves brought from Africa and the West Indies. Generally to be creole means to have some African ancestry, but creole also has a cultural connotation. As C.H. Grant concluded: Creole is "conceived and expressed more as a social and cultural than a biological phenomenon. The concept is therefore used primarily to identify a non-Indian and non-*mestizo* way of life and a set of social values derived, with local adaptation, from the Anglo-Saxon countries, mainly Britain, the West Indies, and from Africa."[6] This definition includes those who call themselves "local whites" who would be excluded by a racially strict definition.[7]

Two-thirds of the country's creoles live in the Belize district, giving first-time visitors to the country the inaccurate impression that creoles form the large majority of the nation's population. In fact, creoles have probably never constituted a majority in Belize, and are now outstripped by the *mestizo* population as the largest ethnic group. In addition to standard English, creoles in Belize speak the creole language, a Belizean *patois*, which passes for a lingua franca in Belize, especially among the youth.

Even after slavery was abolished, creole men continued to dominate the ranks of logging crews, and have historically prevailed in the civil service. As one report argues, "It is the creole who is perhaps most culturally alienated for it was the creole who was slaved, who came in closest contact with the worst evils of the colonizers, and who was most intensely dehumanized, deculturized, and reoriented toward Anglo-Saxon culture and identity."[8] As the group most acculturated to British customs, the creole middle class came to consider itself as the rightful heir of the colonial politics and economy.

An oft-cited example of this acculturation is the fact that the colonial holiday on September 10 to celebrate the Battle of St. George's Caye (where British settlers defeated a Spanish naval force in 1798) gradually became a creole holiday. Evan X Hyde observed: "For the sycophantic creole bourgeoisie class, the 10th represented a legitimization of their supremacy in the civil service administrative circles of government."[9] This identification with all things British, as well as with North American culture, continues to present an obstacle in terms of developing a more integrated and positive sense of cultural identity.

Although the two main political parties seek national constituencies, they are led primarily by creoles. Middle-class creoles and their followers largely supported the British colonial system. In describing creole politicians typical of the English-speaking Caribbean, Trinidadian anticolonial leader Eric Williams scoffed: "They retain little or no trace of their African origin except the color of their skin. . . . They are colored Europeans. . . . in taste, in opinions and aspirations."[10] The PUP, although chiefly a creole political party, extended the existing ethnic-based concept of nationalism to incorporate a multi-ethnic political movement. In so doing, the PUP challenged the racist and elitist attitudes of the traditional creole leadership.[11]

The black consciousness movement in Belize can be traced to the Ex-Servicemen's Riot of 1919 when returning Belizean troops rioted to protest racial discrimination. One of the soldiers, Samuel A. Haynes, helped quell the riot and became a spokesperson for the black troops before the commission of inquiry convened by the colonial governor to examine the cause of the riots. Haynes was a founder in 1920 of the Belize branch of the United Negro Improvement Association (UNIA), a black nationalist movement organized by the Jamaican-born Marcus Garvey. Garvey himself visited Belize and recruited Haynes for work in the U.S. office. The UNIA subsequently lost much of its militancy and became a low-key "friendly society" registered with the colonial government.[12] Affiliated with UNIA were such creole groups as the Black Cross Nurses and the African Orthodox Church. Thus while Garveyism originally promoted the concept that "black is beautiful," it eventually came to promote "black capitalism."

It was not until the 1960s, influenced by black leaders in the United States and Jamaica, that young creoles began seriously rallying around racial consciousness issues. This black power movement reached its height between 1968 and 1970, a period when Evan X Hyde and other creole radicals founded the United Black Association for Development (UBAD), whose constitution was patterned after its UNIA predecessor.[13] The leading organizations promoting creole culture and interests were the Islam Nation Belize, Isiah Morter Harambe Association, and the Afro-Belizean Committee (including Garifunas).

The Rastafarians decorate the cultural fringe of the creole community in Belize. The Rastafarian religion, which came to Belize by way of Jamaica and the United States, is based on the belief that blacks are the reincarnation of the ancient Israelites and that salvation can only come through repatriation to the holy land of Zion through the leadership of a black king.[14] In Belize, as elsewhere, the so-called Rasta are linked more by culture and lifestyle than religion. Few of the Rastas in Belize adhere to the religious dogmas or abstain from red meat. Smoking marijuana is, however, often part of the Rasta culture in Belize.

Largely poor urban youth, Rastas are immediately recognized by their braided dreadlocks. Many are street hustlers, and in Belize City and Caye Caulker they commonly prey on tourists. Locals on Caye Caulker call them "Rastaphonies." A more positive view of these rebel youth is that they are "dropping out of the mainstream Belizean society and adopting the hairstyle of the Rastafari and a philosophy of resistance to this confining economic dependency and mental slavery that is being thrust upon us by new and hostile forces."[15]

Media, based in Belize City, tend to be creole-dominated and to convey the creole point of view. The *Amandala* newspaper, the nation's most influential, is edited by early black power advocate Evan X Hyde, who also runs the popular KREM radio station which in recent years has popularized reggae and "Dance Hall" (rap with a Caribbean rhythm) music.

The cultural myth offered by traditional creole power brokers in Belize is that the country is more culturally and socially linked with the English-speaking Caribbean than with Central America and Mexico. A strong Caribbean link does exist, but over the past 150 years the major cultural and biological influence has come from the country's mainland neighbors. Although the Caribbean connection is mainly perpetuated by the creole sector, many acculturated Latinos in Belize share this viewpoint.[16]

A Spanish-speaking and immigrant culture is deeply rooted in Belize. In the mid-1880s, in fact, there were more Spanish-speaking immigrants in British Honduras than native-born creoles or whites. A population count in 1861 revealed that—mainly as a result of the influx of the War of the Castes in Mexico—47 percent of the country's inhabitants came from Mexico or Central America while only 43 percent were born in Belize.[17]

The persistence of Guatemala's claim to Belize compounds social tensions arising from the influx of Spanish-speaking Central Americans to magnify creole-*mestizo* discordance. In the Mayan and *mestizo* communities, there exist concerns that creoles, long favored by the British in the civil service and police force, will continue to dominate the entire society through control of legal and educational institutions despite their waning population sector.[18] But party politics and the civil service in Belize do not function solely according to ethnicity and culture. As O. Nigel Bolland noted in 1988:

> While a distinct anglophile bias in the institutional structure of Belize has been inherited from the colonial era, this bias has not enabled the creoles to attach their identity to the State in such a way as to attain a hegemonic position over the other ethnic groups, particularly the *mestizos*. This is partly because of the fact that the creoles, though the most numerous group, are nevertheless a minority in Belize, but it is also partly because the colonial legacy of racism has discriminated in particular against black people while favoring those with lighter skins. A light-skinned, straight-haired *mestizo* child who learns English and attends the prestigious St. John's College may be more likely to rise into the elite than a creole-speaking black child.[19]

The Garifuna/Garinagu

In the early 19th century the Garifuna (also called Black Caribs) created a niche in Belizean society. Scattered along the Caribbean coast from Belize to Nicaragua, the Garifuna people initially came to the territory of Belize from the Bay Islands of Honduras.

The Garifunas are a cultural and racial fusion of African slaves, Carib Indians, and a sprinkling of Europeans.[20] With negroid features, a Carib-based language and economic patterns, and strong African cultural traits, the Garifuna are a distinctive mix. The product of what has been called a "voluntary assimilation," members of this hybrid population resisted enslavement but were finally brought under English control in the late 18th century, at which time they were removed to the uninhabited island of Roatán off the Honduran coast.[21] From the Bay Islands, the Garifuna quickly migrated to the Atlantic coasts of British Honduras, Guatemala, Honduras, and Nicaragua. In Belize, they first settled in Stann Creek and soon began working in the logging industry. It is traditionally claimed that they arrived on the shores of British Honduras on November 19, 1802.

Fishing and agriculture are part of the Garifuna tradition, but there is also a strong history of wage labor. Known as exceptional students and linguists, the Garifuna commonly find employment as teachers or civil servants. Several towns, including Punta Gorda and Dangriga, are predominantly Garifuna as are the villages of Hopkins, Seine Bight, Georgetown, and Barranco. The villages of Punta Negra and Mullins River are considered mixed Garifuna/creole settlements. There are also Garifuna concentrations in Belize City and Belmopan, though they constitute less than 10 percent of each city's population. True to their long history of migration, the Garifuna people are spreading throughout Belize as the road network expands and social mobility increases.

The Garifuna community has long struggled to maintain its place in Belizean society. Under colonial rule in the 19th century, they were prohibited from owning land and were considered squatters on land they had farmed for decades. These restrictions against land ownership were designed to create a cheap and available labor force for the logging industry, but the Garifuna consistently resisted attempts to control their labor.

Today, the struggle to maintain their community is largely a cultural one. Although many Garifuna are professed Catholics, they have retained numerous traditions and rituals from their Afro-Caribbean heritage. In the 1980s there was a surge in cultural identity among the Garifuna, with many communities taking steps to foster pride in their customs and language. There is even talk of introducing the Garifuna language into the school system. As part of this cultural revival, it has been suggested that the term Garinagu—their name for themselves—be put into wider public use.

To commemorate their arrival in Belize, November 2 is a national holiday that is widely celebrated throughout the country with music and dancing. At the forefront of efforts to promote the Garifuna language and culture is the National Garifuna Council. The sudden popularity in the early 1990s of punta rock gave the Garifuna cultural identity movement a big boost. A rock adaptation of the traditional call-and-response music of Garifuna women, punta rock enjoyed international exposure following the release of the song "Sopa de Caracol" by a Honduras band. In Belize, "Punta Till You Drop" T-shirts testify to the popularity of this dance music. Created by such Garifuna musicians as Andy Palacio and Pen Cayetano, punta rock carries a message of cultural consciousness. "Uwala, Uwala, Uwala Busingano" (Let's be proud, have no shame) are the lyrics of one punta rock song.

The Belizean Maya

Mayan communities are found in northern, west-central, and southern Belize. For the most part, the Maya who live in Belize today are not directly descended from those natives living in the territory when the Spanish first colonized the region, but rather from immigrants who left Guatemala and Mexico. The Yucatec Maya, who live in the northern districts of Corozal and Orange Walk, came to Belize in great numbers during the mid-19th century to escape the War of the Castes in the Yucatán. Since the 1960s, the Yucatec have gradually been deculturated, many dropping their own language in favor of Spanish and English. Traditional rituals and institutions are largely dismissed as "primitive" and "superstitious," although some efforts are under way to recover the Yucatec language and cultural heritage.[22]

The Mopan Maya, who live in the Cayo and Toledo districts, were historically a lowland group that originally inhabited parts of central Belize and the Petén in Guatemala. Most of the early Mopan in Belize were driven out by the British. In 1886 there was an exodus to southern Belize of Mopan from the village of San Luis in the southern Petén to escape forced labor and taxation. These Mopan eventually founded the village of San Antonio in the Toledo district, which continues to be the largest Mopan settlement. Although their principal concentration is in the Toledo district on the southern flanks of the Maya Mountains, Mopan communities also settled in the towns of San José Succotz and San Antonio in the Cayo district. Culturally and linguistically, the Mopan have more in common with the traditional Yucatec of northern Belize. International and Belizean tourists are attracted to the Deer Dance of the Mopan, which can be traced back to the Classic period.[23] Their economy is a mixture of subsistence crops (beans, corn, roots) and cash crops (honey, cacao, rice). With the growth of the cash economy, Mopan women have become more economically marginalized since most of the cash is earned by the men.

The Kekchí Maya migrated to Belize in the 1870s and 1880s from the Verapaz region of Guatemala to escape their virtual enslavement by German coffee growers. Clustered in some thirty Toledo communities, the largest being San Pedro Columbia, they are the country's poorest and most neglected ethnic group.[24] The Kekchí language is only distantly related to the northern Mayan languages and has few similarities with Mopan. These two Mayan communities even use different words for such common things as the sun and tortillas.[25] Like the Mopan, the Kekchí practice slash-and-burn *milpa* agriculture but are increasingly cultivating cash crops, chiefly rice, citrus, and cacao. They are known for their cooperative work practices, both in agriculture and in community development. Unlike the Mopan who have little contact with the Petén Mopan, the Kekchí maintain contact with their ancestral communities in Guatemala.

In the 1980s the Maya population expanded both in numbers and in diversity with the arrival of thousands of Guatemalan refugees from that country's western highlands. The Maya of Belize do not share a well-defined common cultural tradition. As one scholar noted, "The emergence of a common identity as Maya Belizeans has been slow and imperfect and was more a product of colonial policy than of people recognizing their common heritage and roots."[26]

Stirring in many Mayan communities is a new spirit of cultural revivalism. There is increasing concern about maintaining Mayan cultural identity in the face of the dominant creole and *mestizo* society, which as a whole considers Indian culture inferior and backwards.[27] Although the Mayan communities in Belize have not historically considered themselves part of an overall Mayan entity, in recent years they have recognized the value of establishing common bonds to protect their lands and cultures. But undercutting these new efforts to conserve and protect the Mayan culture is the increased modernization brought by road-network expansion, penetration of radio and television, and the extension of the cash economy. Evangelization by missionary groups also tends to split and deculturate Mayan communities. Some evangelical groups have even preached against the *fajina* tradition of compulsory community participation in village cleaning and maintenance.[28]

The Toledo Maya Cultural Council, established in 1975, was created to protect and project Mayan culture, to defend Mayan rights, and to generate meaningful economic development. Land rights and support for a proposal to create a special Maya Land Trust of some

500,000 acres are also major concerns of the Cultural Council. Responding to charges of cultural separatism, the Cultural Council explained: "In a garden there are many different flowers but they are all part of the same garden. We want to live in unity and cooperation with all Belizeans, but we also want to protect our heritage."[29] To enhance the cause of cultural preservation, plans are under way to create a Maya Institute of Belize.

For the most part, Mayan revivalism has emerged from the less developed and more isolated Indian communities. In the more prosperous areas of the country, particularly the agricultural regions of northern and western Belize, many Indians have shed their traditional culture to overcome the stigma of cultural inferiority and to increase the possibilities of integrating themselves into the economic life of the area. In contrast, in southern Belize many culturally intact villages still exist. The traditional *alcalde* system of Mayan local governance has been recognized in part by the national government, although its autonomy has been undermined by the efforts of both political parties to dominate its activities.

The Ancient Maya

Remnants of the widespread ancient Mayan civilization abound in Belize, but most ruins are covered by a thick layer of jungle green. In Orange Walk District, archeologists have discovered traces of Mayan communities that date back as early as 2000 BC. The Maya flourished until about AD 900, with the population during the Classic Period (AD 250-900) estimated to have been at least 400,000 and possibly much more (Figure 3a).[30] The Mayan centers of Belize were part of a civilization of 3-5 million people that encompassed the Yucatán, Guatemala, and the western reaches of Honduras. Likely inspired by the Olmecs, the ancient Maya established a rainforest civilization—a feat equaled only by the Khmer of Southeast Asia. The Maya regarded themselves—and still do—as products of a great ceiba tree that stands at the center of the universe, holds up the heavens, and is the symbol of all life.[31] Although never managing to harness the wheel to practical use, the Maya's discovery of the concept of zero, the base of modern arithmetic, and their comprehension of the mysteries of time are testaments to the advanced character of their civilization.

Intensive archeological research in Belize during the past twenty years has revealed new artistic treasures left behind by the priests and warlords of the ancient Maya. Diggings and glyph translations have revealed that Belize was home to some of the earliest Mayan settlements. At various times during the Classic period the military power and trading influence of Mayan centers in Belize extended over vast areas in Mesoamerica, reaching the grand Tikal.

The Mayan clusters of this region have been likened to squabbling Greek city-states and warring feudal empires. Rather than viewing themselves as members of a unified civilization, the ancient Maya identified only with their own priests, nobles, and land. Other Mayas, even those living short distances away, were considered foreigners and potential enemies. The idea that all the people of Mesoamerica belonged to a single group was one introduced by the European conquerors.[32] Living in their own city-states, the Maya

Figure 3a
Archeological Chronology of the Maya

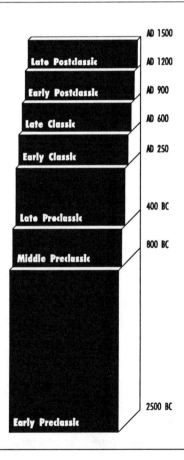

were ruled by dynasties of nobles and priests, who regularly tried to assert their authority over other Mayan settlements. It was a hierarchical civilization of "warlords and maize men."[33] The warlords justified the continuation of their family rule by claiming they brought fertility and prosperity, although in reality it was the peasantry (or "maize men") who sustained the ostentatious spending of their rulers.

From the beginning of Mayan civilization, Belize was part of its heartland. Recent radiocarbon studies confirm that the Cuello site, near Orange Walk Town, dates back to 2500 BC, ranking it as one of the earliest known Mayan sites. Some of the hundreds of Mayan centers in Belize, such as Cahal Pech on the outskirts of San Ignacio, reached their glory during the Preclassic period. As the continuing archeological survey at Caracol has revealed, the Mayan sites in Belize rivaled the most splendid of Mayan cities anywhere. Research also shows that the Maya in places such as Lamanai and Marcos Gonzalez were thriving long into the Postclassic period after many of the Classic centers had already faded or been abandoned.

The reasons why this advanced and ordered civilization disintegrated remain shrouded in mystery. Ecological destruction, demographic decline, internal class warfare, and wars with competing Mayan villages seriously weakened the social fabric. Archeologists speculate that religious centers were abandoned during popular revolts against the religious and political elite. David Pendergast found archeological evidence at Altun Ha that the location's collapse was probably associated with a violent peasant revolt.[34]

An increasingly accepted theory posits that the decline of the Classic Mayan civilization was largely the result of its increasing militarism. Conflicts between neighboring city-states had apparently always existed, but during the Late Classic period Mayan societies turned bloodthirsty. In the ball courts the rubber balls were sometimes replaced with skulls or the heads of prisoners. Although earlier methods of warfare, which emphasized capturing aristocrats and defacing the glyphs that praised their feats, were traumatic (especially for the defeated nobles), there was little mass destruction of lives and property. Such sparring represented merely ritualized conflict between elite troops. More sophisticated weaponry coupled with a new emphasis on the capturing and killing of large numbers wreaked havoc on the civilization. Fortifications were erected as part of the siege warfare that became common in the seventh or eight century. No longer protected by or otherwise benefiting from their allegiance to their autocratic rulers, peasants and workers may have decided to abandon them and their monuments.[35]

The high population density that anthropologists have attributed to the Maya in Belize is not consistent with what the land could have sustained employing simple slash-and-burn agricultural practices. Recent archeological evidence has solved this mystery, showing that at least in northern Belize, Mayan farmers practiced year-round cultivation of wetlands with flood-recessional drainage systems and raised-field agriculture. Seasonal flooding kept soil nutrients high and weed population low, allowing farmers to crop continuously for many years without declining yields. This type of cultivation in the lowlands has the added labor-saving benefit of avoiding forest clearance. In addition to intensive cultivation of wet lowlands, Mayan farmers cropped the uplands during the dry seasons.[36]

The colonial invasion irrevocably changed Mayan societies. Pandemics left thousands dead, while Mayan priests and political leaders were suppressed. In the early 1500s, small Mayan settlements in what is now the Toledo district were overrun by the Spanish, although the invaders never gained a secure hold on the area.[37] In response to demands for a tribute to Spain, the northern Mayan chief Nachankan replied that the only tribute he would pay would be "turkeys in the shape of spears and corn in the shape of arrows." While moving further south, the Spanish encountered similar resistance.

The British, too, set out to subdue the remaining Maya in Belize. Upon encountering resistance, the British colonists organized raiding parties on Indian villages. In 1867, these raids set fire to seven villages and adjoining fields. The last armed resistance of the native population against European conquest occurred in 1872.

Mayan Ruins

Belize has hundreds of Mayan sites, most of them inaccessible and unexcavated. Some of the more important ones are listed below (Figure 3b). Traces of the country's ancient past are also preserved at the Department of Archeology in Belmopan and at the Bliss Institute in Belize City.[38]

Northern Belize

Altun Ha: Located 31 miles north of Belize City at the end of a two-mile feeder road, Altun Ha is one of the most impressive archeological sites in Belize. A major ceremonial and religious center, Altun Ha has two main plazas surrounded by a dozen structures including the Temple of the Sun God, which rises 60 feet. A large water reservoir (inhabited by a 9-foot crocodile) together with the ruin's proximity to the sea help explain its strategic location. Unearthed from one of the tombs, a large jade head representing the Sun God, Kinich

Ahau, is now considered to be one of the country's most treasured artifacts. The accessibility of Altun Ha and its abundant wildlife make it a favorite of tourists.

Marco Gonzalez Site: Located at the southern tip of Ambergris Caye, this Mayan site seems uninhabitable, surrounded by a mangrove swamp and infested with mosquitos. But during its years of habitation, the sea level was much lower, the mangrove swamp was no threat, and the poisonwood that now bothers visitors was nowhere to be seen. Marco Gonzalez probably had a special role in monitoring sea and river access to inland centers such as Lamanai on the headwaters of the New River. Initially without any ties to Marco Gonzalez, Lamanai eventually came to exercise great influence on this caye community. Like the Lamanai Maya, the Maya at Marco Gonzalez weathered the generalized collapse of the Mayan civilization. In fact, Marco Gonzalez, a fishing and shellfish-collecting community, blossomed in the mid-1100s. Between 1150 and 1300 it boasted extensive new construction, perhaps even outstripping Lamanai in per capita richness during this period. Its wealth was a result of its easy living on fish and conch, its lucrative trade in shells, and its role as a transshipment point for goods to the interior. By 1300 the bubble of prosperity had burst, and Marco Gonzalez quickly faded, although it is possible that a few descendants remained when the Spanish arrived in Belize.[39]

Lamanai: Situated on the New River Lagoon, Lamanai (meaning Submerged Crocodile) is known for its longevity and its prominence in the Preclassic era. Its main building, which rises 33 meters, is the largest Preclassic structure in the Mayan area. The 950-acre archeological reserve that encompasses the site preserves the only existing jungle in this area of Orange Walk. Besides the Mayan structures, the reserve also includes the remains of two 16th-century colonial churches and a 19th-century sugar mill. Until its excavation (1974-85), archeologists believed that the Mayan civilization had collapsed and disappeared throughout Belize between AD 875 and 925 But the Lamanai people apparently survived the turmoil of the collapse and maintained their thriving community for several more centuries, albeit without the grandeur of the ancient past. When the Spanish arrived in 1544, they found a viable community still farming around the original ceremonial site.

Other Mayan settlements in northern Belize include: Santa Rita located on the outskirts of Corozal, a site that was probably the ancient Mayan capital of the region and was still occupied when the Spanish arrived; Cerros, a Late Preclassic center of maritime trade situated on the shores of the Corozal Bay; Nohmul (meaning Great Mound), a major ceremonial center located on the Rio Hondo with a massive acropolis from the Late Preclassic period; and the Early Preclassic site of Cuello, with a 70-foot-high temple within the private land of the Cuello Brothers Distillery.

Western Belize

Cahal Pech: Situated on a rise above the western bank of the Macal River just outside San Ignacio in western Belize, this mid-size Mayan center of 34 sites is surrounded by tropical forest. Archeological evidence suggests the site was continually occupied from about 900 BC to AD 800 and may have served as a principal center during the Late Preclassic and Middle Classic periods. In the Early Classic period, the preeminent position of Cahal Pech gave way to Buena Vista, a more imposing site about 6 kilometers away. During the Middle

Figure 3b

Areas of Archeological Interest

1—Santa Rita: Postclassic Mayan civilization.
2—Cerros: Late Preclassic Mayan coastal trading center; Mayan agricultural practices.
3—Nohmul: Mayan settlement area and economic base.
4—Cuello: Earliest Mayan lowland site.
5—El Pozito: Ceremonial center.
6—Colha: Lithic manufacture.
7—Altun Ha: Mayan distribution center.
8—Lamanai: Preclassic Mayan settlement.
9—Moho Caye: Archeological mapping, excavation of coastal Mayan site.
10—Lowe Ha, Sand Hill: Archeological survey.
11—El Pilar, Yaxox, Belize River: Settlement patterns.
12—Barton Ramie: Settlement patterns.
13—Cahal Peck, Buena Vista: Late Classic Mayan communities.
14—Petroglyph Cave: Mayan cave utilization.
15—Xunantunich: Excavation.
16—Cayo, Caracol, Zayden Creek, Pacbitun, Caledonia: Mayan agricultural terracing.
17—Point Placentia: Mayan coastal utilization.
18—Nim Li Punit: Archeological survey.
19—North Spot wreck: Excavation of 17th-century Spanish vessel.
20—Lubaantun: Classic Mayan settlement.
21—Wild Cane Caye: Mayan coastal trade center.
22—Pusilha: Excavation.

SOURCE: Hartshorn et al., *Belize Country Environmental Profile.*

Figure 3b
Areas of Archeological Interest

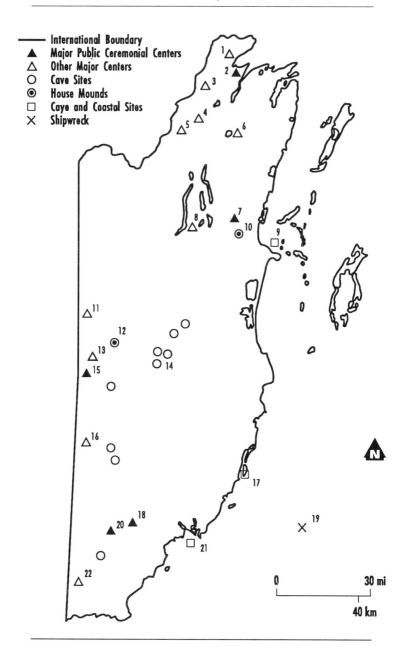

International Boundary
▲ Major Public Ceremonial Centers
△ Other Major Centers
○ Cave Sites
◉ House Mounds
□ Caye and Coastal Sites
✕ Shipwreck

0   30 mi

40 km

Classic period, Cahal Pech (meaning Place of the Ticks) enjoyed renewed prosperity. Yet while other centers continued to prosper, Cahal Peck fell upon hard times and was abandoned by AD 800.[40]

Xunantunich: One of the most accessible of the ancient Mayan settlements, Xunantunich adjoins the present Mayan town of San José Succotz just west of San Ignacio. Though a small site, this Classic period ceremonial center contains a temple called El Castillo, which rises an impressive 130 feet above the jungle floor. The temple-top panorama takes in the green hills of Guatemala and the mountainous Cayo district. Occupied between AD 150 and 900, Xunantunich also offers fascinating stelai and glyphs. Encroaching agriculture and ranching render Xunantunich one of the only remaining stretches of jungle in this area.

Caracol: Deep in the jungle, 50 miles from the nearest town, this isolated Mayan site appears to be the preeminent Classic ruin in Belize. Now overrun by ceiba and cohune palms, it stretches over five square miles with its broad plazas, temples, acropoli, causeways, and residential compounds. Without access to running water, the Caracol community depended on well-engineered reservoirs and practiced terraced farming. Tikal, deep in the Petén department of Guatemala, lies about 46 miles to the northwest through impenetrable jungle. When discovered by *chicleros* in 1936, Caracol was thought to be a minor site but recent archeological excavations show that this Mayan center was larger than Tikal. In fact, in 562 Caracol's Lord Water defeated the warlords of Tikal and dominated the region until about the year 700. Encompassing more tombs and structures than Xunantunich, with one temple rising 137 feet, Caracol may eventually be converted into a 5-square-mile national archeological park deep in the Chiquibul Forest Reserve.[41] It may be reached by an often impassable dirt road from the Augustine Forestry Station in the Mountain Pine Ridge Reserve.

Other Mayan settlements in western Belize include: Pacbitun (meaning Stones Set in the Earth), a major ceremonial center of the Middle Preclassic period located near the town of San Antonio in the Cayo district; and the unexcavated Pilar site, one of the largest Classic centers with 15 courtyards, near Bullet Tree Falls.

Southern Belize

Lubaantun: Perched on a ridge above the Columbia River valley near the Kekchí village of San Pedro Columbia in the Toledo district, Lubaantun (meaning Place of the Fallen Stones) was occupied for only a century or two beginning in the year 700. The 11 structures, all constructed without mortar, depend solely on the precise fit of the building stones to keep them standing. On a clear day a visitor atop the tallest temple (50 feet) can see the Caribbean sea some 20 miles to the east. Although its pyramids (designed with platforms to support wooden structures) do not display carvings, stelai are found in the nearby ruins of Nim Li Punit and Uxbenka. The 1970 excavation of a figurine of a musician wearing a cacao-pod pendant indicates that Lubaantun served as a supply center for cacao beads, which functioned as a type of Mayan currency.

4

Social Forces and Institutions

© Tony Villanueva

Popular Organizing

Without a history of peasant organizing, Belize lacks the kind of poor-people's organizations that have proliferated in the urban slums of other Central American countries. This absence of strong popular organizations is due to many factors: the country's low population density, its less polarized social climate, the availability of land, and a multi-ethnic social composition.

The prominent position of party politics within Belizean society has also tended to fractionalize communities along party lines. Political parties, particularly the People's United Party (PUP), have also had a history of coopting and managing conflictive social issues, thereby obstructing the development of independent poor-people's organizations. At least since the 1950s nationalism has also tended to overshadow class issues in Belize—a phenomenon promoted by both main political parties.

Black Consciousness, Labor Organizing, and Nationalism

The first example of popular organizing in this century was probably the Ex-Servicemen's Riot of 1919.[1] Patriotism for the British Empire swept the Belizean creole community in the early years of World War I and two contingents of black soldiers left for the war in 1915-16. However, they did not go to the front but rather were assigned to work as common laborers for the British expeditionary forces in the Tigris-Euphrates region. Their inferior status as colonial blacks quickly became evident; the British even prohibited them from joining other troops in singing "Rule Britannia." Humiliated and exploited during the war, the troops returned to British Honduras as frustrated, angry men. Upon being denied entry to the Belize City country club and other colonial institutions, the ex-soldiers rioted.

From that riot there emerged a popular leadership and a rising black consciousness in British Honduras, which was heightened by the visit to the colony in 1921 by black separatist Marcus Garvey (see Society and Ethnicity). The local branch of Garvey's U.S.-based United Negro Improvement Association (UNIA) was one of the country's first popular organizations. The anticolonial movement later found its first popular base not within this black consciousness movement, which had become largely conservative and procolonial, but in the labor movement and in the open-air public forums that regularly drew crowds beginning in the 1930s.

World depression aggravated socioeconomic conditions in the colony in the 1930s, resulting in increased social discontent. This unrest manifested its public focus in the Battlefield Park weekend forums where orators would lash out at the colonial government and whatever else bothered them. One of the main orators was Antonio Soberanis, a working-class leader and former UNIA member. In the early 1930s the Laborers and Unemployed Association (LUA) led by Soberanis organized boycotts of merchant houses in Belize City and a strike against the powerful Belize Estate and Produce Company.

Although the LUA disintegrated, partly because of the arrest and imprisonment of Soberanis in 1935, popular anger remained high. Former LUA activists became leaders of the Native First movement, which scored an electoral victory in 1939 on the Belize Town Board. Nationalism was increasingly the major theme of the Battlefield orators. Joseph Blisset, founder of the Belize Independent Party in 1940, called for the expulsion of whites and for union with the United States. Another regular topic at the Battlefield Park forums was the demand for unrestricted adult suffrage, eventually granted in 1954. Belizean novelist Zee Edgell memorializes this time of popular ferment and explosive Battlefield Park oratory in her book *Beka Lamb*, with the protagonist Beka commenting, "Touch anybody nowadays and what do you get? Speech!"

In the 1940s and 1950s politics, nationalism, and populism were all the same element. At the center of this struggle to alter colonial structures was George Price. Price, the personal secretary to creole *chicle* millionaire R.S. Turton, was elected to the Belize City Council in 1947 as a member of the Native First group. Two other important names of this period were Philip Goldson and Leigh Richardson, reporters for the anticolonial *Belize Billboard* and members, with Price, of the same Christian Social Action group. Besides advocating adult suffrage and self-government, these early nationalist leaders called for a "third side" in the Anglo-Guatemalan dispute—namely self-determination for Belizeans. They also founded the People's Committee in 1949 to protest the devaluation of the British Honduras dollar. This committee became the People's United Party (PUP) in 1950.

To extend their popular base, the PUP leaders allied themselves with the General Workers Union (GWU). The middle-class leaders of the PUP soon dominated the labor movement and exploited it for the party's political purposes. Given the anticolonial climate at the time, this seemed legitimate and perhaps necessary, but as a result the unions lost their independence and militancy. When the PUP became the government in the 1960s, the party did not serve its working-class roots. Instead it utilized the Labor Department as a kind of a referee to sort out labor-management conflicts.[2] As a result of internal factionalism and previous cooption by the PUP, modern-day trade unionism is fragmented, disorganized, and virtually powerless (see Labor and Unions).

Cooperativism and Rural Development

Paternalism by the populist PUP also obstructed the emergence of a strong peasant movement. To gain allegiances in rural areas, the PUP government distributed land and formed cooperatives. Since the 1950s the government has periodically addressed the problem of the lack of rural development. The earliest expressions of this concern were the "self-help" projects of the mid-1950s and governmental promotion of rural cooperatives in the 1950s and 1960s. Under the self-help program, the government offered financial and technical assistance while villagers supplied labor for projects to upgrade rural communities, such as the construction of community centers and wells. Credit unions sponsored by the Catholic Church emerged, while the government launched numerous cooperatives by distributing land and offering technical assistance and financing to newly organized community groups. Rural development projects increased in the 1980s primarily due to the injection of funds from foreign governments and NGOs. To take advantage of this new source of funding, there has been a surge in community groups and cooperatives.[3]

The cooperative movement popularized in the 1960s survives in the fishing and agricultural sectors. Although some 125 cooperatives are registered, only half the agricultural cooperatives actually function, while 80 percent of the country's 25 credit unions are still active. Credit unions constitute an important source of loans, providing 7.5 percent of the total credit requirements of Belize.[4]

One showcase story is the Northern Fishermen's Cooperative, founded in Caye Caulker in 1960. Enjoying government protection against foreign investment in the lucrative shellfish and fish export trade, the Northern Fishermen's Cooperative became a resounding economic success, but even here cooperativism is largely limited to sales while production is still handled by individual families.[5]

Most cooperatives formed by the government have failed for lack of marketing know-how, business experience, and technical assistance. One of the more successful cooperative ventures in agriculture is the Belize Federation of Agricultural Cooperatives (BFAC), formed in 1986 to help farmers in Cayo market their crops. In general, though, cooperatives in Belize suffer from poor management, inadequate marketing, and low membership participation. Another weakness of the cooperative sector is the absence of women members and leaders.

Many within the cooperative sector complain that the government does little to provide the technical assistance they need and say that educational programs are necessary to foster a more cooperative spirit in Belize. Community leaders also regret that government and foreign aid programs have accustomed people to expect handouts, and in doing so have undermined the spirit of true cooperativism and collective responsibility that would result in successful and enduring community projects. Another factor in marginalizing the role of cooperatives and village communities in rural development was the government policy in the 1980s of providing cheap food to consumers rather than promoting small-farm development through price and marketing support.[6] The government's strong orientation toward bolstering the agroexport economy also undervalues the contribution of small growers.

Politics and Social Justice

Most social-justice activism in Belize is channeled through political parties. In the 1960s two radical organizations arose to challenge the more conservative political programs of the parties. In 1969 these two groups—United Black Association for Development (UBAD), led by Evan X Hyde, and the People's Action Committee (PAC), led by Assad Shoman and Said Musa—formed a united popular front. But these organizations were short-lived and failed to develop a broad-based progressive social movement.

One result of the ascendancy of two-party politics in Belize has been the politicization of village councils and increased divisions within communities. "Rather than looking after what's good for the village, people just vote for the blue (PUP) or the red (UDP) anymore and we are all divided," observed one community activist in San Ignacio. Village councils replaced the more consensual, nonpartisan *alcalde* system of local governance in many rural areas. In the village of Charlestown (Stann Creek district), social scientist Mark Moberg concluded that "while the *alcalde* was annually elected to his post, the elections were uncontested and served to ratify community support for an impartial and widely esteemed elder."

Symptomatic of the decline in community organizing in Belize has been the demise of *fajina* (work parties), a traditional form of co-operation whereby villagers join together voluntarily on some community project. "It was politics that humbugged *fajina*," said a former Charlestown *alcalde*, "When I was *alcalde* we never thought about politics. Now you can't get a UDP and a PUP to work together, or even talk together."[7]

Party politics has given rise to extreme factionalism even in small villages. Conflicts generally arise not over party ideology but rather over the perceived benefits or spoils the party in power dispenses. A partisan activist in Charlestown commented: "Some years aback we was all brothers and sisters here. Now you want to kill your best bally [friend] for what the politicians them promise you. They break they promise, but we have to live with the poison they spread."[8]

In general, independent popular organizing on a grassroots and community level is weak or nonexistent in Belize. With the increased activity of nongovernmental organizations (NGOs) in the 1980s, the country's civil society gained a valuable new dimension (see Nongovernmental Organizations). In the belief that the lack of basic education is a main reason for community noninvolvement, institutions such as the Society for the Promotion of Education and Research (SPEAR) and the Cayo Center for Development and Cooperation (CCDC) have sponsored a wide variety of popular education and media outreach projects. Out of the incipient environmental movement in Belize, community projects have emerged to protect local habitats as a base for economic development, mainly through ecotourism. But NGOs have thus far failed to realize their potential for instilling community spirit and building collective popular action outside the arena of party politics.

Labor and Unions

Despite steady economic growth since the mid-1980s, unemployment and underemployment persist. Most affected are urban male youth and rural females. There are no reliable figures but 1991 estimates from the U.S. Embassy and the Belize government show a 14-15 percent unemployment rate in the work force of some 60,000.[9] In addition underemployment is consistently quite high because of the large sector of seasonal farm workers. Only about two-thirds of those counted as employed actually have steady, full-time jobs. In the sugar, citrus, and banana industries, many workers who are laid off during slumps tend to return to subsistence farming. The Human Rights Commission of Belize estimates that underemployment is commonly as high as 35 percent. Low labor productivity and the scarcity of skilled labor are among the most salient structural weaknesses of the Belizean economy.

Creating jobs for Belizeans is a major challenge for the government and economy. With an estimated 45 percent of the population below age 14, Belize will in coming years have to increase its ability to generate jobs. Yet there are limits to the job-creation potential of the two leading economic sectors: agriculture and tourism.[10] Although export agriculture as currently practiced is labor intensive, most of the jobs are seasonal and extremely low paid ($7-10 per day). Virtually all the field work is performed by Spanish-speaking laborers, many of whom are either undocumented or in the country under temporary work permits. The tourism industry is booming but is also a seasonal business and directly generates relatively few jobs.

Labor, like other popular sectors, is neither well-organized nor very influential in Belize. Only 12 percent of the work force is organized. Even within unions there is little class consciousness, and strikes are rare. When unions do speak out, particularly the civil-service and teachers' unions, it is more often about political issues than over job-related concerns. High unemployment in Belize City, the seasonal nature of most agricultural work, and ethnic divisions make labor organizing difficult. Also contributing to the depressed state of unionism in Belize is the lack of protection of labor and trade union rights. Although workers are free to join unions, employers are not legally required to recognize a union as a bargaining agent. It is not uncommon for employers to block union organizing by terminating the employment of key organizers. To boost economic growth, the government collaborates with large industries in discouraging union organizing, supplying work permits for cheap foreign workers, and failing to enforce the minimal labor laws that do exist.

The absence of unions coupled with the country's high unemployment rate result in low wages, with skilled workers averaging only $2.50 an hour. Wages for unskilled labor range from 90 cents to $1.25 an hour, with women consistently receiving less then men. The government has acknowledged that "gender bias continues to be a glaring feature of the labor market."[11] The working conditions and low pay of female seamstresses in the textile industry came to public attention during the 1991 strike by the newly organized Women Workers Union. Workers were earning $5.62 a day in piece-work assembly, receiving 30 cents to sew a dozen pockets and 12 cents to iron 12 shirts. The establishment of several new Chinese-owned textile companies and the development of a new export-processing zone in Belize are making such sweatshop labor a base of the country's manufacturing sector.

In 1991 the government established a Minimum Wage Council which proposed to set an across-the-board minimum wage of $1.12, but the business community balked, claiming such a move would discourage new private investment in Belize. All employees in workplaces of two or more workers are covered by social security protections and benefits, although in many cases employers collect income and social security taxes from employees and never report these revenues to the government. Workers are also commonly denied their legally mandated benefits. Fringe benefits for the 45-hour work week add about 15 percent to an employer's wage bills.

Although there is high unemployment in Belize, there are labor shortages in the agricultural sector, the economy's chief realm. The unwillingness of many Belizeans to work in the agricultural sector is partly explained by historical and economic factors. Early on, creoles, blocked from purchasing their own land, tended to seek their fortunes in the cities. Many pursued education as a way to enter the civil service, while others found work as carpenters, blacksmiths, boatbuilders, and repairmen. Also, in part due to the efforts of the country's labor unions, creoles generally refuse to work for the extremely poor wages offered in the agricultural sector.

Rather than participate in the agricultural economy as seasonal laborers or as small farmers, many urban youth, particularly creoles, emigrate or remain unemployed. If the anti-agricultural attitudes of urban Belizeans persist, this crisis of urban unemployment will likely worsen. Transcending an aversion to agricultural labor, unemployment among creole youth appears to be a deep-seated social problem in Belize City—as evidenced by labor shortages in the construction and manufacturing industries despite the high jobless rate. Higher wages in the farm economy and job-training programs targeting urban youth could help alleviate this continuing problem.

Some 1,500 migrant workers enter Belize each year for seasonal work in the banana and citrus industries in the South and the sugar industries in the North. These migrants supplement the domestic supply of seasonal workers, mostly refugees and undocumented Spanish-speaking residents. An investigation by the Human Rights Commission of Belize found that despite existing requirements, higher overtime and holiday pay rates were never paid and there was no proper paysheet system in operation. The Human Rights Commission also reported a lack of health and sanitation facilities, substandard housing, careless aerial pesticide spraying, and polluted drinking supplies. "The situation and conditions resemble the slavery days," stated the report.

Through its immigration policies and work-permit program, the government since the 1960s has ensured a steady supply of cheap labor for the agroexport industries. Defending this effort to meet the labor needs of agroexporters, Minister of Labor Samuel Waight in 1990 explained: "The investor, the person who is spending his hard-earned dollars, makes an assessment of the output of the Belizean worker and the output of the refugee or the foreign worker. And on many occasions it is reported to me that the foreign labor produces more than the Belizean worker. . . . The foreign labor comes in, they're willing to work, do anything below cost, below what our people would normally do. . . . [Because] of the supply and demand situation and the amount of investments any undertaking has, it would be natural for them to try to get the cheapest labor for the highest production."[12] This understanding and solicitous attitude on the part of government also extends to an unwillingness to protect the agroexport industry work force—most of whom are not foreigners but Spanish-speaking Belizeans—from the abusive and illegal labor practices of their employers.

A Brief History of Unionism

Although there had been previous labor disputes, notably the protests of timber industry workers in 1894, it was not until the Great Depression of the 1930s that organized labor became a prominent feature in the country's economic and political life. Its leading figure was Antonio Soberanis, an unemployed mahogany cutter who directed the Laborers and Unemployed Association (LUA), which led the early struggle for workers' rights. The watershed of the labor movement, however, came in 1943 when labor unions, legalized two years earlier, were allowed to organize—albeit restricted by a wartime measure prohibiting strikes in the saw mills. From their lumber industry base, unions gradually spread to many other economic sectors.

As elsewhere in the English-speaking Caribbean, early union activism in Belize greatly contributed to nationalist organizing and the independence movement. Consequently, the country's labor unions and its independence movement became entwined with the PUP, the country's major political party and the focus of the anticolonial struggle. The PUP leaders even shared offices with the General Workers Union (GWU), the country's first major union. In part a result of its links to the independence struggle and the PUP, the growth of the labor movement can also be partially attributed to the involvement of Jesuit clergy in training and education programs for both the GWU and the PUP.

Overall, however, the link between labor and political parties undermined rather than strengthened the union movement. Although the PUP sponsored favorable labor legislation in the 1960s and reached out to workers to expand its political base beyond middle-class professionals and civil servants, the party was uncomfortable with and sought to suppress the class-based militancy of the GWU. Because of its close association with the PUP, the union movement became more a political instrument than a true representative of worker interests. Also contributing to the decline of the union movement were the political splits, inspiring party factions to form their own labor unions. George Price, for example, who in 1952 served simultaneously as president of the PUP and the GWU, supported the breakaway Christian Democratic Union in 1956 after a factional dispute within the PUP.[13]

Following a decade of relative dormancy starting in the late 1960s, there was a resurgence in trade unionism under the banner of the United General Workers Union in the late 1970s and early 1980s. Led at the time by progressive labor activists, the union came to control labor in all the major export industries as well as several government corporations, including the Belize Electricity Board (BEB). Once again, however, political parties in league with the more conservative unions undercut the efforts of the upstart unionists. An anti-communist redbaiting campaign by conservative elements within the PUP and some in the UDP effectively undermined the union.[14]

By the early 1990s, the union movement was weak, demoralized, and badly fragmented. Although the national constitution guarantees the right to join a union, neither the constitution nor the Trade Union Ordinance ensures that a successful union ballot must be recognized.[15] Except for agriculture, transport, and the public sector, union representation is virtually nonexistent. Strikes are rare, and unions exercise little political influence. The entire tourism industry is virtually without union representation, as are the commercial and retail sectors. The country's tiny industrial sector, which includes garment manufacturing, a flour mill, a toilet paper factory, a few breweries, and a cigarette manufacturing plant, also has no unions.[16]

The Trade Union Congress, the country's leading labor confederation, receives foreign assistance through its Trade Union Institute and affiliated unions from the American Institute for Free Labor Development (AIFLD), a U.S.-government-funded organization. A prominent member of the Trade Union Congress, the Public Service Union (PSU) represents the country's junior and middle-level civil servants. Other unions associated with the Trade Union Congress are United General Workers Union (which represents citrus industry and Dangriga dock workers), Belize National Teachers Union, Belize Electricity Workers Union, Belize Telecommunications Workers Union, and the Belize Workers Union (representing citrus and sugar workers). Of less importance are the Christian Workers Union and the Democratic Independent Union.

Schools and Education

The quality and availability of public education in Belize compare favorably with most other nations of Central America. Primary school education is free and compulsory for all children to age 14, with girls constituting 49 percent of primary school and 52 percent of secondary enrollment.[17] Student/teacher ratios are good by world standards: 25 students to one teacher in primary schools and 13 to one in secondary and postsecondary institutions. Although the official literacy rate stands at 90 percent, the Ministry of Education acknowledges that 70 percent is a better estimation.

Education receives the largest share of the national budget, and the government appears intent on further improving public education. Another encouraging sign is the growth of preschool education, with preschools increasing from 31 in 1980 to 75 by 1989.[18] Nevertheless, high absenteeism and dropout rates, poor teacher education, and insufficient funding of schools plague all levels of public education (Figure 4a).

Church schools form the foundation of the country's educational system, with less than 10 percent of the 247 primary schools operated by the government. The colonial government budgeted only small sums for public education, leaving the job of educating Belizean children to the churches. It was not until the 1950s when the nationalist movement bloomed that allocations for public education substantially increased. But rather than developing a national system of state-operated schools, the government has opted to subsidize the church schools. Under this system tax revenues cover 100 percent of the salaries of primary school teachers and 70 percent of high school teacher salaries. However, it is the church administration that hires and fires these teachers.

This system of government-subsidized denominational schools dates back to 1816 when the Church of England founded the country's first public school. Three denominations—Anglicans, Roman Catholics, and Methodists—administer most of the country's primary schools, although in recent years evangelical churches such as the Assemblies of God have been opening more schools. The Roman Catholic Church alone administers about 60 percent of the church-run schools in Belize. The government's role in the church-administered schools is largely limited to paying teachers' salaries and providing other financing. There is a significant discrepancy between rural and urban schools, with the former hampered by lower-quality teachers and facilities. While some 50 percent of urban primary students pass the National Selection Examination (for entrance to secondary school), only 20-30 percent of rural students pass this exam.[19]

Although primary education is free, there is a high rate of nonparticipation. Of the approximately 80 percent of Belizean children registered in primary schools, only 55 percent complete the full eight-year cycle, with more than half of the attrition taking place in the first two years. Secondary education is still more restricted.[20] Less than two-thirds of those entering high school complete the four-year cycle at the nation's 30 secondary schools. Eight of the high schools are operated by the government while the balance are managed by churches. All primary and secondary education in Belize follows the British examination system whereby students are required to pass standardized exams before proceeding to another level of schooling. Only a tiny elite continues on to a university, and only 13 percent of Belizeans have received professional or technical training.[21]

Issues of Higher Education

The two largest postsecondary institutions are the privately owned St. John's College Sixth Form and the government's Belize Technical College Sixth Form. Limited sixth-form education has recently become available in Dangriga and Corozal. These sixth-form schools offer two-year academic courses leading to associate degrees.

Higher education is also offered at the Belize Teachers College, the School of Nursing, and the Belize School of Agriculture—all administered by the government. In 1979 the government established the Belize College of Arts, Sciences, and Technology (BELCAST). The intent was to create a national university that would coordinate all postsecondary institutions and eventually offer a bachelor's degree. BELCAST proponents in the PUP hoped that the new school would form the foundation of a four-year institution of higher learning owned and controlled by Belize, and associated with the University of the West Indies. From the beginning BELCAST was more a vision than an actual university, functioning much as a coordinating committee of postsecondary institutions and creating conflict when it directly absorbed the Belize Teachers College.[22]

Controversy over the direction of higher education in Belize continued when the UDP government decided to abort BELCAST and replace it with the University College of Belize (UCB). Opting to co-sponsor its project for higher education, the UDP government in 1986 established UCB as a two-year college administered by Ferris State University in Grand Rapids, Michigan. In the opinion of UDP Minister of Education Derek Aikman, a partner relationship with a U.S. institution would raise the standard of education while guaranteeing the integrity of UCB degrees. But BELCAST supporters argued that the arrangement with Ferris State undermined the country's sovereignty. Rather than developing an indigenous educational institution according to the original BELCAST design, the country's higher education was being entrusted to a U.S. university.[23]

The deal with Ferris State formed part of a larger trend of increasing U.S. influence in Belizean culture and society. In addition to its role at UCB, Ferris State also organized a program to train the administrators and principals of all the country's secondary and primary schools. Exchange programs with Murray State University in Kentucky and the University of Northern Florida added a further dimension to the expanding U.S. influence in Belizean education.

By 1991 the partnership with Ferris State had disintegrated. From the beginning the Ferris State administrators of UCB had pledged that UCB graduates would be granted joint degrees from UCB and Ferris State University. The Ferris State administration finally acknowledged what many had long suspected: it had failed to obtain official recognition for the UCB degrees in the United States.

Figure 4a

Education in Belize

Literacy	70%
Children benefiting from preschool programs	9%
Disabled children receiving special education	10%
Children completing primary school (8-year cycle)	55%
Children completing secondary school (4-year cycle)	10%
National budget spent on education	24%
Education budget spent on teachers' salaries	93%
Primary school teachers meeting Ministry of Education standards	44%

SOURCES: *Education in Belize: Toward the Year 2000* (Belize: SPEAR, 1991); Ministry of Education statistics; World Bank, "Belize: Education Sector Review Report" (January 1989); UNICEF, *Position Paper, 1992-1996.*

Responding to UCB student and alumni concern, PUP Minister of Education Said Musa promised that the Belizean government would continue to recognize the validity of UCB degrees and that it would seek recognition of UCB course work by individual U.S. universities. The PUP government announced that it would continue funding UCB, open an additional campus in Belmopan, and seek to renew previous attempts begun with BELCAST to establish cooperative relationships with other educational institutions in the region, especially with the University of the West Indies.[24] The Ministry of Education also plans to broaden the UCB curriculum, which under Ferris State focused almost exclusively on business administration and secondary education. Despite its problems, UCB has expanded the opportunities for higher education in Belize, with its student body more than tripling in its first four years.

Room for Improvement

Under Said Musa's previous tenure as education minister, the Ministry developed social studies and history textbooks that addressed such issues as racism, imperialism, and international trading relationships. These high-quality, provocative textbooks remain popular despite the UDP government's attempt to suppress them.

Although the education system in Belize compares favorably to others in Central America, there remains much room for improvement. Functional literacy is much lower than the official figure, which reflects little more than a familiarity with the alphabet and an ability to write one's name. Due to a shortage of qualified teachers, the student/teacher ratio rose during the late 1980s. Other problems include the nonstandardization of curricula and the lack of sufficient funding for adult instruction, technical training, and higher education. Also striking is the complete lack of bilingual education in such a multilingual society.

Broader concerns about the educational system in Belize include the dangerous mixture of education and politics as well as the involvement of churches in public education. The government has promised to promote an education system that nurtures "open and enquiring minds in our children" and which "plays a central role in developing the country's potential."[25] Yet there is an underlying concern that churches, which are faith-based and patriarchal, may not be the best instruments to encourage such critical and open-minded thinking. Although dual control over education has created standardization and efficiency problems, any attempt to change the church-state collaboration would stir up a storm of community opposition and political dissent.

Communications Media

Although the media has never been severely repressed in Belize, the government's traditional aversion to criticism and its attempt to control the electronic media have constrained free circulation of information and ideas. The PUP, which criticized government restrictions on the media as a major part of its successful 1989 campaign, moved swiftly after its election victory to fulfill its campaign pledge to encourage a more open media policy with unrestricted political dialogue.

The PUP government formed an independent media authority called the Broadcasting Corporation of Belize (BCB), similar to the British Broadcasting Corporation, which oversees the country's TV and radio stations. Entirely free of government control, the BCB is directed by an 11-member board, appointed jointly by the minister of broadcasting, the leader of the opposition party, Chamber of Commerce leaders, the Trade Union Congress, and nongovernmental organizations. With the government's encouragement, the Belize Association of Media Organizations (BAMO) was established in 1990 to protect the interests of the media. An association of journalists formed in early 1992.

Soon after the 1989 elections the PUP-controlled legislature abolished the offense of criminal libel, under which the editor of the *Belize Times* was repeatedly charged in 1987 and 1988.[26] Although the PUP government has earned good marks for its media policy, it was criticized for its failure to rescind an ordinance that gives the minister of finance broad discretion regarding which information is allowed to enter the country.[27]

There are at least four weekly newspapers that hit the streets of Belize City each Thursday or Friday, and most copies are gone by the weekend. Despite the wide variety of newspapers, the quality of reporting is poor, although steadily improving. News accounts are few and skimpy, often bordering on slander. Most papers present an undisguised political slant. *The Reporter*, owned and edited by UDP member Harry Lawrence, is the most business-oriented paper, often expressing the positions of the Chamber of Commerce and Industry. *Amandala*, the country's most politically independent paper, is owned and edited by Evan X Hyde, the 1960s leader of United Black Association for Development whose personality, controversial opinions, and love of sports are all reflected in his paper's pages. The official voice of the UDP is the *People's Pulse*. Its counterpart is the *Belize Times*, which serves as a PUP mouthpiece. There is also a small weekly newspaper in San Pedro called the *San Pedro Sun*. In an effort to reach out to the Spanish-speaking community, both *The Reporter* and the *Belize Times* run articles in Spanish, and the government's magazine *Belize Today* is now a bilingual publication. Newspapers are rarely circulated outside Belize City.

The country's newspapers carry little or no international news but are teeming with name-calling and back-and-forth accusations. The *People's Pulse* blasts PUP leaders as "moguls of the Perverted Useless Party" and dubs party chair Said Musa as "Mendacious Musa." In turn, the PUP's *Belize Times* assails the UDP with equal gusto. The only source of serious independent analysis is *Spearhead*, a periodical published by SPEAR (Society for the Promotion of Education and Research). Although making no effort to disguise its leftist views, *Spearhead* tries to steer clear of interparty political conflicts and concentrate on more long-term issues. SPEAR also publishes collections of academic studies called *Spear Reports*, drawn from a selection of papers presented at the annual Studies on Belize Conference that SPEAR sponsors.

Belizean Studies, written by the Belizean Studies Association at St. John's College, is an excellent journal designed to disseminate research on Belize locally as well as to provide an outlet for Belizean research and writing. Another such avenue is provided by Cubola Publications, which publishes both fiction and nonfiction works by local authors. *Belize Currents*, an appealing glossy magazine designed to attract tourists and investors, began operations in 1989 from its offices in Houston, Texas. The monthly *Belize Review*, edited by Meb Cutlack and billed as a source of "news, views, and ecotourism" information, is closely associated with the tourism and real estate industry and publishes many classified ads for beach and ranch property to lure foreign buyers.

As recently as the early 1980s, radio was probably the country's most influential medium. Radio Belize, the country's first station, broadcasts in Spanish and English. Renamed Belize Radio One by the UDP government, it is the only electronic media to reach the entire nation. Eventually, the PUP government approved a longstanding application by Evan X Hyde, owner of the *Amandala* newspaper, for a new radio station called Radio KREM. Promoting local music talent,

Radio KREM quickly became very popular and has contributed to the revival of radio in Belize.

In the 1980s radio was largely supplanted by television as the country's favorite medium. By 1991 there were four television transmitting channels, including stations run by the BCB and the Catholic Church. Several other applications for channels are being considered, including one from the Kremandala organization. Although Washington protests the widespread pirating of U.S. programs by numerous private cable operators, the audience for such pirated programming continues to expand.

The government requires that at least 2 percent of TV broadcasting be local programming, but a lack of resources and training has inhibited production of programs locally. Recently, however, the BCB has been producing documentaries and other programs. *Belize All Over*, a half-hour program produced by Great Belize Productions, broke new ground when it aired a series of short, lively vignettes about life in Belize, featuring culture and entertainment as well as interviews with writers and politicians. Given the void of government support for local television programming in Belize, it has been difficult to produce anything other than advertising. In the more open climate following the 1989 PUP victory, though, a weekly interview program hosted by young leaders in each political party made its debut.

Health and Welfare

Mobile clinics are just one indication that health care in Belize is a far cry from what is found in neighboring Central American countries. Although health statistics in Belize are not on a par with the industrialized world, Belizeans generally enjoy good health and access to health care facilities (Figure 4b). Government policy holds that health services should be democratic, comprehensive, educational, participatory, and accessible.[28] The government even recognizes that good public health is a function of improved socioeconomic conditions. The Ministry of Health's 1990-1994 plan notes that "the promotion of health is dependent on the equitable distribution of land, food, education, housing, recreational facilities, access to roads, and other means of communication." The Ministry is committed to meeting the World Health Organization's goal of "health for all by the year 2000," through the use of a Primary Health Care Strategy, emphasizing community participation.[29]

Health care in Belize falls far short of these ideals, but a combination of foreign aid (mostly from UNICEF and AID), an educated citizenry, government commitment, and the contributions of nongovernmental organizations has gone far to improve the country's health services. About 75 percent of the population has access to government medical facilities, which include seven public hospitals, rural clinics, and mobile clinics. However, about half of rural inhabitants still lack easy access to health services.[30] A valuable government program trains selected villagers as rural health promoters, and includes in their training a course on medicinal plants and natural healing.

The widespread access of Belizeans to potable water is a major reason for their comparatively good health. Almost the entire population in the eight main urban areas is supplied by public water systems, with 62 percent enjoying home connections. In rural areas, about 50 percent of residents have easy access to potable water. There are sewage systems in Belmopan and Belize City.

The state of health has steadily improved largely as a result of primary health programs instituted in the late 1970s and early 1980s. One improvement has been a downward trend in mortality, with crude mortality falling from 6.2 per thousand to 4.2 per thousand, and infant mortality falling from 29 deaths per thousand live births in 1980 to 20 per thousand in 1990. In certain areas of the country, including the Toledo and Belize districts, there exist pockets of higher infant mortality. Although the situation is much improved, easily preventable infectious diseases continue to be a major health problem.

Belize is relatively free of epidemic diseases, although malaria persists as a leading cause of hospital admission, especially in the Punta Gorda district in southern Belize. Though not as severe as elsewhere in Latin America, the incidence of malnutrition, especially in rural areas and among the refugee population, is still troublesome, registering 8 percent for those children under age one and 19 percent for ages one to four. Dietary habits and poor weaning practices are

Figure 4b

State of Health, 1990

Mortality rate/1000 people	4.2
Infant mortality rate/1000 live births	20.2
Population growth rate	2.7%
Population under 15	45%
Fertility rate (three times higher than other Caribbean nations and about equal to Central American nations)	5.2 children
Population doubling date	2011
Life expectancy	70
Easy access to potable water	80%
Urban	100%
Rural	53%
Adequate sanitation facilities	43%
Urban	60%
Rural	21%
Population without access to health facilities	25%
Incidence of malaria (1989)	3285 cases
Physicians per 1000 people	5.1
Number of hospitals	9

SOURCES: Ministry of Health, *National Health Planning System 1990-1994* (Belize City: PAHO-WHO, November 1990); UNICEF, *Program Position, 1992-1996*; Ministry of Economic Development, Central Statistical Office, *Abstract of Statistics* (Belmopan: November 1990).

the principal causes of nutritional deficiencies; only half of the country's infants are exclusively breastfed for the recommended four months, and an estimated 55 percent have marginal vitamin A deficiencies. Almost half of the women registering at prenatal clinics show signs of anemia.

The number of children born to single women is increasing, from 43 percent of all live births in 1970 to 57 percent in 1988, with babies born to unmarried women in Belize City constituting 67 percent of all births. Forty-six percent of mothers bear their first child before they reach the age of 19, and 27 percent of all Belizean households are headed by women. Largely because of pressure from the churches, the government has no national family-planning policy or program. In 1991 UNICEF warned: "The trend of a growing child population, coupled with growing refugee and immigrant populations, heavy migration of the economically active population to the United States and a life expectancy of 70, could make Belize essentially into a nation of children, elderly, and the poor."[31]

Although the health care system in Belize compares favorably with other countries in the region, it is not devoid of problems. The principal obstacle to better health care has been the lack of adequate government financing. Unfortunately the social services sector in Belize is deteriorating as the per capita provision for social services continues to decline. In keeping with the conservative financial programs of the previous administration, the PUP government has curbed its public-sector commitments. In the 1986-90 period, the health sector percentage of the total budget remained static, the social services share decreased, and only the education sector expanded. The government's budget for health would need to be dramatically increased for the country to extend health care beyond primary programs to chronic and curative care, which is now seriously deficient and available for the most part only in Mexico.

The country's nursing school teaches Belizean nurses the techniques of primary and preventive health care, but nursing pays poorly, so many nurses leave the country to seek higher-paying jobs in the United States. This, together with the great strain on services imposed by refugees, has created a critical shortage of nurses in rural health posts. Although the number of Belizean doctors is increasing, most are based in Belize City, leaving other district hospitals without the capability to perform surgery.[32] Lack of medicines and funding plague government hospitals, so many Belizeans seek health care and cheaper medicines in Mexico.

Church and Religion

In Belize, the dominance of the Catholic Church was achieved not as a result of Spanish colonialism but rather through immigration from Mexico and the development of a strong church infrastructure by U.S.-based Jesuits. The flight of refugees from the Yucatán began in 1848 during the War of the Castes and formed a solid base for the Catholic Church in Belize, which has diversified into a religious institution encompassing all races and cultures. The strength of the Catholic Church in Belize is largely attributable to early outreach work by the Jesuits, who now administer five of the country's 12 parishes and the prestigious secondary school, St. John's College. Roman Catholics constituted almost 70 percent of the population in 1970, falling to 62 percent in 1980 and steadily decreasing since then to perhaps as low as 50-55 percent by the early 1990s.[33]

The Anglican Church, which established a diocese in Belize in the early 1800s, is the leading Protestant denomination, claiming some 12 percent of the population, followed by the Methodists with 6 percent. During the last 15 years, both the Catholic Church and mainline Protestant churches have lost members to new evangelical sects, led by the Assemblies of God. Converts are also swelling the ranks of such fundamentalist churches as the Baptists and Seventh Day Adventists. Other U.S.-based religious groups increasing their presence in Belize include Jehovah's Witnesses and the Church of Jesus Christ of Latter-Day Saints (Mormons).

Assisting the evangelical churches are an array of nondenominational Christian organizations, all based in the United States, that sponsor evangelical campaigns, feeding centers, church-building projects, and medical and dental programs. These include Youth With a Mission (YWAM), Campus Crusade for Christ, Feed the Children/Larry Jones' Ministries International, Christian Medical Associations (coordinated by the Southern Baptist Mission), Amigos International, and Compassion International.

Since independence, the evangelical boom has been one of the most striking changes in Belizean society. Bible institutes, corner churches, schools, media programs, and a wide range of social service projects sponsored and financed by U.S. evangelical churches are altering the country's social fabric. Yet evangelical growth in Belize is not as dramatic as in other Central American countries. Evangelical missionaries lament that the arrival of television in the early 1980s dramatically reduced interest in evangelical conversion as people generally prefer to stay at home in front of their TVs than to attend religious services.

Other denominations in Belize include the Old Colony Church and the Evangelical Mennonite Mission Church. In Belize City there is a small Nation of Islam community whose members publish the occasional *Jihad* tabloid.

Nongovernmental Organizations

Nongovernmental organizations (NGOs) first became a feature of Belizean society in the 1960s mainly in the form of church-related bodies and charity groups. It was not, however, until the 1980s that private organizations began proliferating. This mushrooming of NGOs was due in part to an outpouring of foreign funding following independence but was also the product of a rising consciousness in Belize about the role and potential of private organizations in society.

CARE, the first U.S. NGO to establish operations in Belize, remains one of the largest. As in other countries, CARE directly coordinates its health and development projects with the state. By prior agreement with the government, CARE concentrates its health projects in the North, Project Hope locates in the Central region, and Project Concern International works in the South.

Among the leading U.S. NGO recipients of Agency for International Development (AID) money are Project Hope, CARE, International Executive Service Corps (IESC), Project Concern International, Partners of the Americas, Cooperative Housing Foundation (CHF), Florida Association of Voluntary Agencies for Caribbean Action (FAVA/CA), Pan American Development Foundation (PADF), American Institute for Free Labor Development (AIFLD), Heifer Project, Joint Agriculture Consultative Corporation, and Volunteers in Technical Assistance (VITA).

In addition, AID has funded an array of local private organizations, including the Belize Agri-Business Company (BABCO), Belize Chamber of Commerce and Industry, Belize Tourism Association, Belize Family Life Association (associated with Planned Parenthood International), Breast is Best League, Parents' Resource Institute for Drug Education (PRIDE), Belize Enterprise for Sustained Technology (BEST), Council of Voluntary Social Services (CVSS), and National Development Foundation of Belize. Much of this U.S. support for local organizations began drying up by 1991. NGO activities in Belize are also sustained by such foreign foundations and agencies as the Canadian International Development Agency (CIDA), Canadian University Students Organization (CUSO), Inter-American Foundation, and Oxfam-Mexico.

A frequent criticism leveled in Belize is that little NGO attention has been directed to community development training or popular education. Although the proliferation of NGOs in the 1980s resulted in measurable improvement in health and business promotion, NGOs have as yet made little headway in sparking broader social development and sustainable rural development. There is also a concern that the influx of foreign NGOs and funding has encouraged dependent attitudes rather than promoting a sense of self-determination and local problem solving. At the same time there is a recognition of the valuable contributions of foreign NGOs and the critical importance of foreign assistance. In that regard, the cutback of AID funds for NGOs and social services raises fears that many important health, family planning, and other service projects will not endure.

As NGOs expanded in Belize, the government demonstrated keener interest in their operations. At a 1988 meeting with the government's Inter-Ministerial Committee (IMC), NGOs made three requests: 1) that the government recognize other NGO umbrella organizations beyond the well-established but conservative Council of Voluntary Social Services, 2) that there be regular interchanges between NGOs and the government, and 3) that there be clear and impartial guidelines regarding NGO rights and operations so as to avoid favoritism and political victimization.[34] In response, the PUP administration has increased cooperation and joint planning between government and NGOs. A new NGO coordinating body was formed—the Association of National Development Agencies (ANDA), comprising Belize Agency for Rural Development (BARD), Help for Progress, Belize Federation of Agricultural Cooperatives (BFAC), BEST, and the Society for the Promotion of Education and Research (SPEAR).

One of the first activities of the NGOs associated with ANDA was to cosponsor a workshop in March 1990 with the Ministry of Economic Development to discuss NGO participation in the government's development plan. The NGOs recommended that the government increase its support to local producers, strengthen the Belize Marketing Board, institutionalize mechanisms for improved government/NGO coordination, and establish a framework to improve community involvement in the planning process.

As one of the few organizations to focus on popular education, SPEAR defines itself as a "nonpartisan organization dedicated to creating national consciousness and achieving social and economic justice for the poor and powerless majorities through research, popular education, organizing, community development, and social action." SPEAR has established an impressive documentation center in Belize City and sponsors occasional forums to discuss current local and international issues. In 1990 the government invited SPEAR to coordinate a national literacy task force, and it now sponsors a radio call-in program. A similar group in the Cayo district, the Cayo Center for Development and Cooperation (CCDC), also sponsors popular education projects.

Supplementing the above NGOs is a panoply of smaller groups, ranging from the Belizean Assembly for and of Disabled Persons, to the Center for Environmental Studies. Yet despite the greater NGO presence following independence, civic activity in Belize remains largely passive and is characterized by individual rather than collective action. Continuing clientelism by the government and political parties has the effect of discouraging nongovernmental problem solving.

Women and Feminism

Although women's organizations are nothing new in Belize, historically they have been chiefly church-related, charitable, and civic
groups, rather than women-oriented advocacy or service organizations.[35] As in many other third world countries, the United Nations
declaration of 1975-1985 as the International Decade of Women
sparked the emergence of a women's movement in Belize.

Today there are a half-dozen organizations concerned with
women's rights and needs, ranging from a rural-development group to
one concerned about violence against women. In government, there is
a Department of Women's Affairs as well as a government-sponsored
National Women's Commission. Since 1982 the women's movement
has sponsored a week of educational events to celebrate International
Women's Day (March 8). The theme of recent activities was "Women
+ Men = The Key to the Future." The Belize Women Against Violence
(WAV) regularly present a Women's Liberation Award to honor out-
standing Belizean women and to raise public awareness about the
many contributions of women to Belizean society.[36]

The late 1970s was a fruitful time for women's consciousness, cul-
minating in 1979 when a group of activists led by Regina Martínez
and Cynthia Ellis founded the first women's concerns organization,
Belize Organization for Women and Development (BOWAND). At the
end of its first decade, BOWAND, located in a wooden house in Belize
City—"My House"—continues to sponsor projects that not only improve the socioeconomic conditions of urban women but also broaden
awareness of women's issues throughout the country. Among its activities are an annual women's wellness fair, self-help health care
education, skills training, and a women's art exhibition. Pursuing
grassroots activism, BOWAND also organizes women into economic
collectives, urging them to work cooperatively to confront their common burdens of unemployment or underemployment.

Two of BOWAND's founders became especially concerned about the needs of rural women and concluded that a separate organization was needed to deal with their problems and concerns. In 1985 they officially launched the Belize Rural Women's Association (BRWA), based in Belmopan. BRWA collaborates with a number of groups in the outlying districts to deal with work-related issues, and it tackles the special health problems faced by women in rural areas, where health services are meager. BRWA publishes a quarterly newspaper, *The Belize Woman*, which reports on the organization's projects and activities.

Founded in the 1980s, Women Against Violence (WAV) has made great strides in raising public consciousness about the seriousness of battering and rape in Belize. Because of the efforts of various women's organizations, women are now talking more about the issue and reporting abuses to the police. WAV is promoting a range of legislative measures regarding violence against women, which remains a chronic problem in Belize. Existing statutes permit the introduction of testimony regarding a woman's past sexual activity as a rape defense and do not recognize the category of marital rape. Similarly there is no legal protection for women in common-law marriages.

Belize also has several organizations that focus on family planning and child/maternal health, including the Breast is Best League (BIB) and the Belize Family Life Association (BFLA). However, abortion, which is illegal in Belize, is available only from lay practitioners, and according to the Belize City Hospital is the sixth most common reason for hospital admission and the third leading cause of hospital morbidity.[37] Although the Ministry of Health does not recognize abortion as a cause of death, a survey by the Pan American Health Organization and the World Health Organization ranked abortion as the number one cause of death among women in Belize.

Leaders of women's organizations complain of extensive job discrimination and unequal pay levels facing Belizean women, many of whom are family heads. Virtually all the workers in the country's expanding garment industry are women. Enduring sweatshop conditions, they earn about $1.10 an hour—even less than the $1.25 minimum for unskilled labor. Income-generation data from UNICEF show that 76 percent of female employees earn less than the average annual income as opposed to 59 percent among males.[38] Typically, laws requiring lunch breaks and overtime pay are ignored, apparently with the approval of the Ministry of Labor. The terrible conditions and low wages in these garment shops have sparked labor protests, such as the formation of the Women Workers Union in 1991. In addition to their underemployment, women—particularly those under 20—suffer higher unemployment than do men.

Women are relegated to roles as organizers, vote-getters, and food providers for the country's political parties. Since independence in 1981 not one of the ministers in any of the three governments has been a woman, and only one female has served in parliament.[39] Working to correct this imbalance is the Women's Political Caucus (WPC), founded in 1991 with membership from both political parties and various women's groups.

A BRWA organizer discussing the major concerns of the women's movement observed that Belizean women still undervalue themselves. "It's a lot of work," she said, "in getting women to see that what they feel, what they have to say, or what they think is important." According to BFLA director Jewel Patton-Quallo, "The bottom line is economic. Women not being independent so that they can stand on their own is a big problem." Reflecting on the past 15 years of women's organizing in Belize, activist Diane Haylock noted that organizers have learned to reach out to grassroots women on issues that directly affect and concern them. She also observed that increasing communication between women's organizations in all countries sharpens each group's awareness about a wide range of women's and feminist issues.

Immigration and Emigration

The ethnic make-up of Belize is in constant flux. Successive waves of Central American immigrants are evidenced by the frequency of Spanish-speaking street vendors, bilingual Stop/Alto signs, and the increased availability of tamales. Besides joining the ranks of the country's booming informal sector, the immigrant population can be found clearing their *milpas* (corn patches) in the Maya Mountains or working as temporary laborers picking oranges or cutting cane. Since land ownership is not an option for illegal immigrants, most either squat on bush land or rent or sharecrop farms. They perform the hardest and worst-paid agricultural work, and are scattered throughout the country in at least 80 villages.

In the Corozal and Orange Walk districts, Salvadoran and Guatemalan immigrants have replaced the Mexican "*arrochos*" who previously cut sugar cane during the annual *zafra*. Many have gathered in the Cayo district, either in small villages or in the Valley of Peace settlement sponsored by the United Nations. In Stann Creek they form the backbone of the citrus and banana industry. Refugees from Mayan communities in Guatemala have relocated in the many isolated villages in the southernmost district of Toledo. There are no firm numbers on the population of refugees and displaced persons, but a conservative estimate in early 1992 set the number of refugees at 30,000 and the number of displaced persons at 10,000.[40] Other estimates put the total as high as 50,000. They all constitute part of what is sometimes called the "alien" or "Spanish" issue in Belize.

Aware that the country needs a larger population to develop economically, Belize historically has welcomed immigrants. Through the early 1980s the country maintained an open-door policy toward those with a background in agriculture and who were interested in contributing to the development of Belize. Labor shortages in agriculture partially explain the PUP's willingness to assimilate refugees from El Salvador and Guatemala. However, critics of the PUP contend that its generous policy of allowing these new arrivals to settle on state land also served to bolster the party's political base.

Salvadorans have been emigrating to Belize since the 1930s, and Guatemalans have long been trickling across the border to escape economic misery and political violence. But due to escalating repression and war in the region after 1979, a torrent of Central Americans flowed into Belize, obligating the government to seek assistance from the United Nations High Commissioner for Refugees (UNHCR). Some refugee families were given uncleared parcels of forested land in what has come to be known as the "Valley of Peace" area near Belmopan. The government also extended public services such as health care and education to the recent immigrants. Other refugees established satellite communities on the outskirts of urban centers. One such cluster of Guatemalans and Salvadorans on the edge of Belmopan is known as Salvapan.[41]

In 1984 the government began to implement measures to control the influx of Central Americans. It announced an amnesty for all undocumented residents as the first step in establishing a system to document all non-Belizeans. With the transfer of government from the PUP to the more creole-based UDP, an even more restrictive immigration policy was enacted.[42]

By the mid-1980s popular resentment, particularly among the creole population, began to build against the so-called "aliens." The UDP government fed this growing sense of resentment and suspicion in an apparent effort to stir up nationalistic support for the party. Treatment of refugees reached its nadir in 1987 when the government's Immigration Advisory Committee recommended that Belize reject the United Nations Convention on Refugees. The committee observed that "should the Belizean government wish to treat Guatemalan refugees differently from other refugees this will not be in accordance with the Convention." Adding its voice to the antirefugee discussion, the Foreign Ministry, which handles immigration matters, proposed in 1987 that the role of the UNHCR in Belize "be reduced and eventually phased out."[43]

Tensions eased by the late 1980s, and beginning in 1989 Belize began to work more closely with the UNHCR in an effort to coordinate policy on a regional basis. In May 1989 the government participated in the International Conference on Central American Refugees in Guatemala City, which resulted in a number of recommendations about ways to improve conditions for refugees and displaced persons. In 1991 the government did finally sign the 1951 UN Convention on Refugees. There remains, however, continuing immigrant resentment over the government's insistence that refugees be subject to deportation unless their status is officially recognized and registered. Ignorance, fear, and their remote location from any immigration office prevent many undocumented residents from registering even though they might have valid claims to be political refugees.

Although the hysteria about the "aliens" has diminished, widespread concern persists that the new immigrants are altering the social balance of the country. By 1991 there were signs that the government and the Belizean public were again turning less tolerant of the new immigrants. Reports revealing that approximately one in five residents was a refugee or displaced person from El Salvador or Guatemala raised new concerns about the society's changing ethnic balance and the ability of the government to provide services for all these immigrants. At an international conference on Central American refugees in early 1992, the government said that the "social, political, and economic costs" of its refugee policy were becoming increasingly apparent, noting that the "high proportion of refugees may result in ethnic polarization, potentially resulting in instability."[44]

About half of all Belizeans now speak Spanish as a first language. Despite new efforts to incorporate the Central Americans and to educate Belizeans themselves about the multi-ethnic character of their society, anti-Central American sentiment is still prominent. Newspaper and radio reports tend to sensationalize crimes committed by the "Spanish" as being symptomatic of the violent and barbaric nature of all Latin societies. As a result, Spanish-speaking immigrants are often victims of discrimination and targets of racial epithets.[45] Those without proper papers are commonly short-changed by employers.

Its large immigrant population poses serious social and economic problems for this tiny nation. Although Belize has done more than many neighboring governments for its refugee population, the illegal influx of Central Americans has severely strained limited government resources and has been a cause of serious social tension.

Leaving for the USA

While receiving immigrants from several directions, Belize is simultaneously being drained by emigration. Since World War II, a steady stream of Belizeans have packed their bags and headed to the economic colossus of the North. At least 60,000—or one of every five—make their permanent home in the United States.[46] More than half enter the United States illegally, either by arriving without proper documentation or by overstaying their nonimmigrant visas.

Migration northward began during World War II when more than a thousand Belizeans were contracted for agricultural work in the United States to meet the labor shortages caused by the war. This foreign worker program was the first and only time Belizeans emigrated for agricultural work. After the war, they set their sights on the Northern cities hoping to find industrial jobs created by the post-war economic boom. This "pull" of economic opportunity continues to draw Belizeans to the United States. Although its standard of living contrasts favorably with that of its neighbors, Belize is an economic and cultural backwater compared with the United States. The tiny country, even in the best of times, cannot offer its young women and men the kind of wage, educational, and vocational opportunities available in the United States. Lured by the chance to live in an industrialized developed nation, many Belizeans leave their underdeveloped homeland behind for the lights of New York, Los Angeles, Chicago, and Miami. Although living outside their country, émigrés do make an important contribution to the Belizean economy. Remittances in the 1981-86 period averaged $21 million annually or 12-15 percent of the GDP.

The "pull" of opportunity in tandem with the "push" of underdevelopment create a compelling motivation to emigrate North. Housing shortages, low wages, high unemployment, and a limited educational system are among the conditions that push Belizeans toward the United States. But the country's alarmingly high rate of emigration cannot be explained entirely by economic factors. The ever-more-pervasive U.S. culture (imprinted upon Belize by television, tourism, and trade) seduces Belizeans to reject their own country for the lure of the cultural mecca to the north. Also contributing to the pull northward are the vivid accounts from family members of higher wages and better access to material wealth.[47]

Creoles, and to a lesser extent Garifunas, have been the country's primary emigrants, constituting an estimated 75 percent of the Belizean population in the United States.[48] During the 1980s women outnumbered male emigrants. Although no one factor explains this proclivity of creoles to emigrate, their English-language skills certainly facilitate their ability to assimilate and find good work.

5

The Environment

© Tom Barry

Conservation and the Environment

For most of Belize's history, "the environment" has meant little more than "the bush"—vast stretches of tropical forest to harvest for logwood and mahogany, and later *chicle*. Belize was the land of lumberjacks whose saws bit into all but the most remote primary forests. The lack of a road network limited their reach as did the rugged terrain of the Maya Mountains. Fortunately the timber industry in Belize—the main source of export income until the 1950s—did not clearcut timber but selected only the logwood and valuable hardwoods, leaving much of the forest canopy intact.

The Baymen left behind a dual environmental legacy. On the one hand, the logging industry leveled most of the hardwood growth and violated all but the most inaccessible primary forests. However, unlike an agroexport plantation economy that would have required an extensive road system and would have completely cleared the forests, the loggers relied on waterways to float felled timber to the coast, leaving much of the country relatively untouched by modern development (Figure 5a).

Belize has an opportunity to avoid many of the mistakes that have wreaked such environmental and economic havoc elsewhere in the region. Unlike developed countries at the curative stage in environmental conservation, Belize can still employ primarily preventive measures to preserve its eco-stability. Its low population density and relatively high educational and income levels combined with the fact that such a high percentage of the land remains under at least partial forest cover allow Belize a chance to chart a new course of sustainable development. The challenge facing the nation is to advance economically while recognizing the ecological boundaries of economic progress.

Deep within these tropical forests are more jaguars than in any other Central American country. Also found are large communities of endangered howler monkeys, tapirs, and scarlet macaws, along with

700 native tree varieties and 533 species of birds.[1] Environmental initiatives in the 1980s by both the government and private organizations have resulted in new nature reserves, legal protections for the

Figure 5a

Environment in Statistics

Total population	235,000 (1992 estimate)
Population density	10 persons per sq km
Population growth rate (including immigrants)	5%
Population growth rate (without immigrants)	2.7%

Land use

Total land area	22,965 sq km (8,867 sq miles)
Original forested land (potential without human interference)	90%
Broadleaf closed forest	74%
Pine open forest	5%
Mangrove and swamp	11%
Actual extent of forest cover	70%
Forest with potential for tree harvest	7%
Land suitable for mechanized agriculture	19%
Land being used for agriculture	15%
Land being used for agriculture/ranching	2%
Reserves (public and private) as % of total land	32%
Percent of reserves that are protected	20%
Percent of logging production coming from reserves	40%
Annual deforestation rate	3-5%

Biodiversity

Flowering plants	4000 species
Birds	533 species (33 threatened)
Mammals	155 species (15 threatened)
Reptiles	107 species (7 threatened)
Native trees	700 varieties
Orchids	72 varieties

SOURCES: Overseas Development Administration, *Belize Tropical Forestry Action Plan, Report to the Government of Belize* (London: September 1989); H. Jeffrey Leonard, *Natural Resources and Economic Development in Central America* (Washington: International Institute for Environment and Development, 1987); Hartshorn et al., *Belize Country Environmental Profile*, p. 21; AID, *Natural Resources Management and Protection Project* (Belize: July 1991); UNICEF, *Position Paper, 1992-96.*

environment, and an expanded environmental consciousness among Belizeans. But the booming tourism industry, expanding agroexport production, new population pressures, and the drive to accelerate the country's pace of development threaten Belize's land and sea environments. Although the government has at least rhetorically joined the conservation bandwagon, its commitment to ensuring clear water, stopping illegal dumping, restricting dangerous pesticides, providing sewerage services, and pursuing appropriate land-use policies is not as evident.

Belize is perhaps the only country with a joint Ministry of Tourism and Environment, reflecting the booming ecotourism industry. The PUP government, while upgrading its tourism infrastructure, collaborates with environmentalists to promote the ecotourist attractions of the country. The sometimes conflicting interests between conservation and tourism promotion surface over plans to extend the country's transportation network to make isolated areas of Belize more accessible to tourists. Tourism leaves in its wake increasing boat pollution, waste disposal problems, environmental degradation of the cayes, and motor traffic. Developers have begun combing every inch of Belize, examining its investment potential for tourism. Previously unvisited forest wilderness and small cayes are now being explored by an ever-expanding number of ecotourists.

Mainland Environmental Issues

Although Belize has taken important steps to conserve its natural environment, primarily by creating protected reserves and parks, its overall economic development strategy does not in practice integrate a strong environmental perspective. The country has no land-use strategy and no legislation requiring environmental impact studies prior to major development projects. The agriculture sector is not guided by the principles of sustainable growth but rather by profit margins and the dictates of the market. Inappropriate agricultural practices, soil erosion, pesticide contamination, and continuing deforestation result from short-sighted economic development schemes.

The three main classifications of land in Belize are national or crown lands, forest reserves, and private or freehold lands. Despite what one might expect, national lands and forest reserves can be sold or leased to private developers, local or foreign. Private land sales, however, are regulated by the Aliens Landholding Ordinance of 1973, restricting non-nationals to half-acre lots within urban areas, unless special permission is granted by the Ministry of Natural Resources. About 37 percent of land in Belize is privately held, 34 percent is national land, and 29 percent is in publicly owned forest reserves (Figure 5b). Private lands include several protected reserves coming to 3.5 percent of total lands. National lands include leased lands, amounting to 10.5 percent of total land tenure, and reserves for the Amerindian population, which account for 1.5 percent of national territory. National forest reserves include national parks and protected reserves, which represent 3.5 percent of total land.[2]

Private land is highly concentrated, with just 2 percent of the estates constituting 85 percent of total private holdings. On the bottom end, 86 percent of the titles amount to less than 5 percent of total private land.[3]

The transfer of land from forest to agriculture is accelerating in Belize despite recent additions to the country's forest reserves and national park system. Both agroexport and *milpa* slash-and-burn cultivation are responsible for this continuing loss of forested land—with deforestation as high as 5 percent annually. Hunting and *milpa* farming are not necessarily antithetical to sustaining biodiversity, but under present cir-

Figure 5b
Land Tenure and Ownership

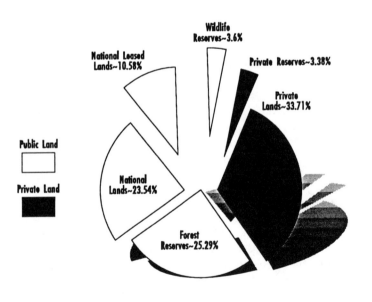

SOURCE: Belize Center for Environmental Studies, 1991.

cumstances wildlife and plant life are not being given sufficient time to regenerate because of increased population pressure.[4]

Expansion in the citrus industry has resulted in the planting of orchards on fragile hillsides and in unsuitable soil. In the 1980s citrus groves extended to some 1,400 acres of forested land, only 400 acres of which had soil suited for citrus development.[5] The result has been soil erosion, drainage problems, deepening gullies (in the Cayo district), and low productivity. The government does require land-use permits for converting forest land to agriculture but the granting of those permits is usually perfunctory with no requirement for a study of soil suitability. Increasing citrus cultivation, mechanized rice farming, cattle grazing, and *milpa* agriculture present the leading deforestation threats.

Pesticide and fertilizer contamination is a growing problem in Belize. Traditionally, small farmers have used few chemical inputs but recent immigrants from other Central American nations are accustomed to higher levels of pesticide applications. Most chemical use, however, is by the main agroexport industries. This has become not only a natural resources issue, but an increasingly severe occupational health problem for farmworkers and their families. Aerial spraying commonly blankets streams as well as farmworkers and their homes near the plantations. The workers and their families use the streams flowing through these agroexport estates for drinking and washing. Most acute is contamination from the banana industry, which requires large amounts of chemical inputs and irrigation. Highly toxic pesticides and fertilizers are often applied in heavy doses to irrigation water at the very time when stream flows are at their lowest and least able to dilute the poisons. The government has no standards for testing pesticide residues in beef or crops, and itself uses DDT and malathion for malaria control.

The government has a well-publicized land-acquisition policy that essentially encourages new development projects without consideration of their environmental impact or sustainability. Land concessions and tax exemptions are routinely granted with no prior investigation of the optimal use of the land. Political and economic motives rather than environmental planning generally guide such land-use decisions as new road construction or the transfer of reserves to agricultural production.

The government has numerous programs to provide credit, promote investment, and facilitate marketing for agroexport production. Without regulations that prioritize sustainable development practices, these promotional programs tend to encourage excessive use of chemical inputs, increased use of agricultural machinery that compact fragile soils, and intensive agricultural practices that cause stream siltation and water contamination.

As in most developing countries, the main problem is not the lack of protective regulation but rather the implementation and enforcement of laws already on the books. Mindful of its lack of personnel and fearful of inhibiting economic activity, Belize rarely enforces its regulations with fines or even warnings. Inspectors do not regularly respond to reports of river contamination, unlawful defoliation near stream beds, or toxic waste dumping. Six years after its creation in 1985, the Pesticide Control Board levies only an occasional fine while contraband imports of pesticides, including restricted and prohibited chemicals, continue unabated.

Of the "dirty dozen" poisons indicted by the Pesticide Action Network as the most damaging to human health and the environment, Chlordimeform, Paraquat, and Methyl Parathion are routinely used in Belize. While restricted, applications of DDT, Pentachlorophenol, and HCH/BHC are not uncommon.

There are no fines for damaging the regeneration potential of forests, and the Forestry Department exercises little control over trail or road building in national reserves. One obstacle is the lack of sufficient staff: a forestry contingent of 24 guards cannot adequately monitor over 8,000 square miles of reserves, seven fisheries agents cannot patrol all inland and coastal waters with their two patrol boats, and the one-person hydrology department cannot mount a serious water-quality control program.

Clearing of vegetation along river banks is prohibited but is regularly done by agroexporters and *milperos*. Coupled with the cultivation of inappropriate lands, riverbank farming increases siltation, which in turn may be damaging the coastal reef as rivers dump silt and pesticides into the sea. Beginning in the late 1980s residents of the cayes began to observe mile-long plumes of silt flows off the northern shores. A related problem is the absence of major reforestation programs in either the private or public sectors.

Water Quality and Marine Issues

Although rainfall is abundant and rivers and streams crisscross the country, water quality is rapidly becoming a major environmental concern. The government has no monitoring program to assess water contamination by agriculture and industry. Villages are not required to treat their water sources, and development concessions are issued without testing water quality at the proposed site.

Because so much of the population lives on the coast, it is one of the most heavily impacted areas. Among the many coastal environmental issues, the loss of mangrove habitats is perhaps the most critical. To make room for hotels, industrial development, and beachfront housing, mangroves are being removed, resulting in serious beach loss and soil erosion in the developed cayes and in populated coastal areas, particularly around Belize City. Developers view mangroves and the sea grasslands that extend from the coast and the cayes as useless and unsightly. But these ecosystems anchor sand and provide some protection against hurricane losses. After the mangroves were removed from Caye Chapel resort to create beaches, the island developers subsequently had to build sandbag walls in a desperate attempt to forestall accelerating sea erosion. Mangrove habitats also suffer from trash dumping, unregulated gravel mining (resulting in siltation), and erosion of cayes and coastal beaches from unrestricted sand mining.

Unbridled development on Ambergris Caye and, to a lesser extent, Caye Caulker threatens the sustainability of the tourist trade. Water availability and waste disposal are now pressing problems on those two cayes. No longer can the islanders simply dump their trash outside the towns or let the sewage flow into the sea, and the large tourist trade is siphoning off the limited supply of drinking water. Septic tanks are not an answer since the porous coral sands allow sewage to seep into the ground water.

To meet export and tourist demand, lobster and conch harvesting appear to have surpassed maximum sustainable yields, with local fishermen routinely supplying restaurants with undersized lobster.[6] Restaurants also commonly serve exotic dishes like turtle meat, tempting even the most environmentally conscious tourists. A conch hatchery operating in San Pedro produces a negligible yield, and if the sea conch population is to recuperate, a respite from the present levels of harvesting is needed.

Although the reef and seagrasses are still in relatively good condition, they are threatened by the booming tourism industry and by siltation and pesticide runoff from the mainland. A related problem is eutrophication resulting in algae accumulation especially on the leeward side of the cayes. To remedy these and other problems, the government created a Coastal Zone Management Unit within the Fisheries Department. The coastal management zone includes the coastal plain extending to the barrier reef and three atolls located in what Belizeans call "the blue" or the deep sea: Lighthouse Reef, Glover's Reef, and the Turneffe Islands. But the management plan is handicapped by underfunding, lack of monitoring, and lax enforcement. Marine reserves such as Hol Chan have been established but some fishermen boast that they still harvest those waters. During its first year, the reserve monitors issued no citations or fines.

Janet Gibson, president of the Coastal Zone Management Unit, estimated that 30 percent of the pollution in Caribbean waters results from recreational boating, with both small launches and cruise ships dumping garbage and releasing gas and motor oils into the sea. Increased dredging by sea resorts to create marinas and beaches (and the subsequent dumping of spoils into mangrove habitats) also worry the coastal management unit. As a result of this destruction and pollution, wetlands are dying off—along with the wildlife that depends on them.[7]

National Parks and Reserves

In the 1920s the colonial government woke up to the fact that uncontrolled logging was ruining the country's economic base. In 1924 it enacted an ordinance that created a Forestry Department and set regulations for timber harvesting on crown and private lands. For the first time forest reserves were delineated, but this was done on the basis of geography and availability rather than by technical analysis. In 1954 the government declared a new forestry policy that set guidelines for sustained-yield harvesting while making provisions for a wide range of environmental conservation measures. What the forestry law did not do was establish implementation procedures for these strongly worded policies—a problem that persists in the 1990s.

It was not until the 1960s that Belize began to consider establishing national parks and protected areas. Sparking this new environmental consciousness was the destruction caused in 1961 by Hurricane Hattie. Belizeans began understanding for the first time that their natural resource base was limited and fragile. Several small protected reserves, including the Columbia Forest Reserve and the Guanacaste National Park, were created and placed under the management of the Belize Audubon Society. However, it was not until 1981 that a national parks system was initiated and Belize began to set aside new protected lands. From humble beginnings, this effort gained momentum in the late 1980s with the support of international conservation organizations. By early 1992 there were 14 national parks, protected reserves, and special development areas (Figs. 5c and 5d).

The Belize Audubon Society with assistance from a wide range of international conservation organizations manages most of the government's national parks and protected reserves established under the National Parks Act. It also manages on an interim basis the bird sanctuaries and parks, mostly small unpopulated cayes, established under the Crown Lands Ordinance.[8]

In addition to these protected public lands, several private reserves were established in the 1980s. The Community Baboon Sanctuary spans several creole communities along the Belize River and was created by the locals to protect the black howler monkey. As much as possible, the natural habit is maintained for the some 1,200 monkeys (called baboons in Belize) living in the area, and hunting is prohibited. This effort has proved so successful that other communities in Belize (for example, those involved in protecting sea turtle eggs on Ambergris Caye) and around the world have adopted the baboon sanctuary as a viable model for integrating conservation with local community life. Another prominent private reserve is the Shipstern Nature Reserve where butterflies are bred and exported to parks and tourist centers in Britain and other countries.

However, parks have been created in a haphazard fashion rather than as part of a planned environmental strategy. For the most part, they are the result either of an effort to preserve individual species

Figure 5c

Parks and Reserves

Parks and protected reserves

Half Moon Caye	1982
Crooked Tree Wildlife Sanctuary	1984
Cockscomb Basin Wildlife Sanctuary	1986 (expanded 1990)
Blue Hole National Park	1986
Hol Chan Marine Reserve	1987
Guanacaste National Park	1990
Bladen Branch	1990
Five Blue Lakes National Park	1991
Laughing Bird Caye	1991
Chiquibul National Park	1991

Special development areas

Monkey River	1991
Manatee	1991
Corozal District East	1991
Burrell Boom	1991

Private reserves

Ix Chel Farm and Tropical Education Center	1983
Community Baboon Sanctuary	1985
Society Hall Nature Reserve	1986
Rio Bravo Conservation Area	1987
Shipstern Nature Reserve and Butterfly Breeding Center	1988
Monkey Bay Wildlife Sanctuary	1990

and their natural habitats (the red-footed booby at Half Moon Caye and the jaguar at Cockscomb, for example) or of the acquisition of land that might otherwise have been developed in an environmentally detrimental way.[9] This type of ad hoc planning may change if the government adopts proposals to identify vulnerable vegetation/habitat types rather than individual species in need of protection.

Big-game hunting associations in the United States have been petitioning to open the country again to jaguar hunting. But there is rising sentiment among Belizeans that commercial jaguar hunting is not in the country's best interests. A report commissioned by Wildlife Conservation International found that Belizeans living in areas populated by jaguars now look upon them with pride as a living symbol of the country. Communities near the Cockscomb Basin jaguar reserve are vocal in their appreciation for the environment and wildlife, and they are outraged by the thought of wealthy foreigners hunting their jaguars.[10]

Attracting the Ecotourist while Conserving the Environment

Beyond its alluring reputation for sea and sun, Belize offers the ecotourist and local alike a wide range of outdoor adventures and nature experiences. With the exception of the major tourist spots (Ambergris Caye and Caye Caulker), most of the nature reserves are not easily accessible. Unless you have a four-wheel-drive vehicle, the only way into the Cockscomb Basin reserve is a 6-mile hike backpacking all your food since there are no stores. To reach the Ix Chel Farm, where you can take the Panti Trail and learn about medicinal plants, you paddle a canoe two hours up the Macal River. In addition to offering foreign ecotourists a jungle vacation, the country's new reserves and parks have served to dramatically increase local interest in conservation. Among the wide range of reserves created in the 1980s are the following:

Hol Chan: The Maya phrase for "little channel," Hol Chan is a marine reserve established in 1987 near San Pedro on Ambergris Caye. Extending from the mangrove swamps through the seagrass bed offshore to the reef, this 5.5-square-mile reserve has proved so successful that another reserve is being planned for the Caye Caulker area further south along the same reef. The reserve, a favorite for snorkelers, has gradually gained the support of local fishermen who initially regarded it as a loss of important fishing ground. Marine biologists have discovered that species valuable to the local fishing industry are proliferating within the reserve and on its periphery. By protecting a portion of the reef, the reserve acts as a nursery since

Figure 5d
National Reserves

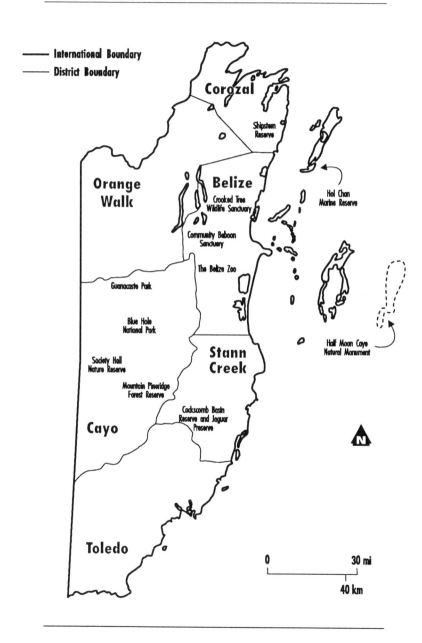

International Boundary
District Boundary

Corozal

Shipstern
Reserve

Orange
Walk

Belize

Crooked Tree
Wildlife Sanctuary

Hol Chan
Marine Reserve

Community Baboon
Sanctuary

The Belize Zoo

Guanacaste Park

Blue Hole
National Park

Society Hall
Nature Reserve

Mountain Pineridge
Forest Reserve

Stann
Creek

Half Moon Caye
Natural Monument

Cockscomb Basin
Reserve and Jaguar
Preserve

Cayo

N

Toledo

0   30 mi

40 km

most reef fish tend to be sedentary and long-lived, their fertility increasing with age. As young fish spill over the reserve, they can be sustainably harvested. "We've seen a big increase in commercial species—spiny lobsters, queen conch, and groupers," reported Hol Chan director James Azueta.[11] Thanks to strict protection, Hol Chan is among the few of some 300 marine sanctuaries around the world that seem to be achieving both conservation and economic development. Its success may have important implications for reef conservation and fisheries management not just in Belize but throughout the world.

Belize Zoo and Tropical Education Center: Although not a reserve, the Belize Zoo, established in 1983, has markedly improved conservation awareness in Belize. The zoo contains 70 indigenous rainforest species—many of them orphans left in the wake of an abandoned documentary film project. Located about 30 miles west of Belize City on the road to Belmopan, the Belize Zoo is home to April, a tapir who has become a favorite of the thousands of Belizean schoolchildren who visit the zoo annually. "The zoo is the most important environmental tool in the country," said James Nations of Conservation International, "because so many people see animals and learn respect for them, and it makes them less likely to destroy their habitat."[12] Zoo founder Sharon Matola, known as the "zoo lady," believes the zoo helps combat destructive local myths about wildlife—such as the belief that tapirs can use their noses to skin people alive. A yellow-headed parrot greets visitors with a repeated "hello," and a handwritten sign designed to discourage the popular practice of taking birds for pets reads: "I am very noisy. I am very noisy every day. I live to be 50 years old."

Bladen Branch Reserve: This 135-square-mile forest reserve in southwestern Belize is home to more than a hundred species of mammals, 350 species of birds, 750 species of trees, and 1,500 species of flowering plants. Its endangered animals include the jaguar, ocelot, jaguarundi, Margay cat, black howler monkey, and Central American tapir. The area is so pristine that the biologist studying the forest said that in order to sleep, earplugs are needed to dull the cacophony of chirps, shrieks, and howls that rise from the jungle at night.[13]

Rio Bravo Conservation Area: This 152,000-acre reserve in northwestern Belize is administered by the Program for Belize, originally a project of the Massachusetts Audubon Society but since 1990 also registered in Belize as a nonprofit corporation. The conservation area was originally part of a 700,000-acre tract of land that Belizean businessman Barry Bowen had purchased from the Belize Estate and Produce Company, a lumber company that once was the colony's largest private landholder. In 1986 Bowen divided the tract into three parcels and sold two of them, one to two Houston speculators and another 193,000-acre tract to Coca-Cola Foods. Faced with the threat of a worldwide boycott over plans to turn part of its tract into a citrus plantation, Coca-Cola abandoned the idea and divested all but 50,000 acres. Program for Belize bought a 110,000-acre plot from Bowen with financial help from the Nature Conservancy, AID, and other foreign organizations and individuals. Together with 42,000 acres donated by Coca-Cola, this rainforest constitutes the Rio Bravo Conservation Area which is held in trust for the Belizean people by Program for Belize. The plot purchased by Houston investors Walter Mischer and Paul Howell is now operated as the Yalbac Ranch and Cattle Company, which in addition to cutting hardwoods also cultivates citrus and produces beef. Once baseline studies are complete, the tract will be operated as a biosphere reserve that will coordinate economic development projects ranging from ecotourism and limited timber extraction to the harvesting of nontimber forest products. According to Program for Belize, the emphasis will be on sustained-yield production and responsible management mindful of the interests of Belizeans for centuries to come. A Program for Belize representative observed, "It's encouraging to have a situation so full of potential. Belize holds enormous possibilities to develop innovative land-use techniques. If this country plays its future right, in 20 or 30 years Belize could become a developed nation in complete control of its natural resources."[14]

The Role of Private Organizations

Organized environmental lobbying and education by citizen groups date back to the founding in 1969 of the Belize Audubon Society (BAS), the country's first environmental nongovernmental organization (NGO). Although the impetus for its founding came from a U.S. expatriate, its governing board is composed mainly of Belizeans. Until 1973 the BAS was closely linked to the Florida Audubon Society, but it later disbanded its membership and program committees. In fact, for the most part the BAS functioned more like a social club for birdwatchers than an activist environmental group with conservation expertise. The presence on the five-member board of two sisters and one brother-in-law of Prime Minister Price lent the group special influence.[15] Due to this political connection and because the government itself did not have the capacity, the BAS was named guardian of several of the country's earliest protected zones.

During the late 1970s several foreign environmental organizations played a role in improving natural resource conservation in Belize. In 1978 a consultant for the UN's Food and Agriculture Organization (FAO) drafted the nation's first wildlife and national park legislation. This was followed in 1979 by a survey of marine reserves by the International Union for the Conservation of Nature, and an effort by the World Wildlife Fund and Wildlife Conservation International in support of wildlife protection projects in Belize, including financing the acquisition of Half Moon Caye as a national park.

With independence in 1981 the government expanded its commitment to protecting natural resources and wildlife. Two key pieces of legislation—the National Park System Act and the Wildlife Protection Ordinance—formed a legal base for the establishment of national parks and the regulation and restoration of wildlife. As before, the management of the newly created national parks was entrusted to the BAS since the Department of Forestry lacked adequate financial and technical resources to handle the job. Yet the BAS also lacked the staff, skills, and financing needed to manage the expanding national park system successfully. Its directors, for the most part, were not environmental activists, nor did they have the technical expertise necessary for such a task.

International environmental organizations, especially from the United States, dramatically increased their activities in Belize during the 1980s. A two-year study of the nation's jaguar population sponsored by Wildlife Conservation International (an arm of the New York Zoological Society) paved the way for the creation of the Cockscomb Basin Wildlife Sanctuary near Victoria Peak. Recognizing the potential for wildlife protection and rainforest conservation in Belize, the Massachusetts Audubon Society, together with a grouping of Audubon associations called the Audubon Alliance, began directly funding the BAS, enabling it to evolve from a purely volunteer organization into a more professional one with full-time staff.[16]

Also in the early 1980s a coalition of U.S. conservation groups formed that included the National Audubon Society, Nature Conservancy, World Wildlife Fund, Wildlife Conservation International, World Resources Institute, and Massachusetts Audubon Society. Under the name of Friends of Belize (FOB), this loose coalition hoped to coordinate conservation funding in Belize, envisioning the creation of a sustainable environmental reserve. The sale of the vast Bowen tract of rainforest land in northwest Belize to Coca-Cola and to two U.S. businessmen spurred Friends of Belize into action.

Whereas other more radical groups demanded a boycott of Coke, a few FOB partners negotiated with the corporation to ensure that the development would not unduly damage the Belizean environment. Out of their dealings with Coca-Cola emerged a plan sponsored by the Massachusetts Audubon Society that established a large reserve of land covering 152,000 acres, merging the purchase of 110,000 acres from Belizean businessman Barry Bowen with 42,000 acres donated by the company itself.

Another new environmental organization is the Belize Center for Environmental Studies (BCES), established in 1988 to sponsor research and educational programs. It has compiled an extensive library and data base on the Belizean environment and has published textbooks and children's coloring books on environmental themes. Its main focus, however, is promoting sustainable resource and land-use practices, and it advocates that environmental impact assessments be required before any major private- or public-sector development project is initiated.

Earth Day was celebrated in Belize for the first time in April 1990, reflecting a broad base of concern for the environment. Symptomatic of this heightened environmental consciousness was the formation of new activist organizations such as the Youth Environmental Action Group in San Ignacio. Under the umbrella of the national government, the Belize National Environmental Council was established in 1990 as a consulting group for government policy and a coordinating mechanism for all conservation activities. It includes NGO representatives, business people, and representatives from the main government agencies involved in conservation. Also contributing to environmental education are the Belize Zoo and Tropical Education Center and the Ix Chel Farm.

Other foreign groups involved in conservation in Belize include the Wild Wings Foundation and the John D. and Catherine T. MacArthur Foundation. Official bilateral funding comes largely from the U.S. Agency for International Development (AID), and Peace Corps volunteers provide additional assistance. AID also directly funds local environmental NGOs, such as Program for Belize, a joint Belizean-U.S. organization directed by Belizean Joy Grant and financed by AID and several U.S. environmental groups. Not only are foreign organizations financing environmental studies and sponsoring new reserves in Belize but they are also working closely with government to increase its planning and management capability. For example, World Wildlife Fund enabled the Forestry Department to establish a Conservation Division, and through AID's Resource Management Project the government is expanding its institutional capacity to protect the environment.

Beyond Conservation

Sensitive to criticism that traditional conservationism ignores the need for economic development, many conservationists advocate a multidimensional approach that incorporates profit-making activities within forest reserves. Protection of natural resources and economic development are not necessarily incompatible. In fact, the commitment to protected reserves that maintain or restore biodiversity might make good economic sense for all sectors of society.

Economic development projects typically degrade natural environments, resulting in decreased potential not only for ecotourism but for sustainable exploitation of natural resources. Instead of declaring all natural environments off limits to economic development, some groups, both foreign and local, are lobbying for the creation of public and private "biosphere reserves." With an emphasis on sustainable production, these groups hope that economic development projects could continue indefinitely without destroying the natural resource base.

Various types of nontimber forest products lend themselves to environmentally sound economic activities. Even limited timber cutting could be sustained without destroying biodiversity. Increasing demand from Japan for *chicle* (gum base), logwood (for dyes), and orchids point to the great potential for forest products. Demand is also escalating in Europe and the United States for orchids, *izote*, and medicinal plants. Other possibilities include allspice, rubber, natural oil resins, nuts, and copal incense, all products of the tropical forest. Advocates like Joy Grant of Program for Belize insist that nontimber forest products are "worth far more than declining crop yields from slash-and burn agriculture," adding that there needs to be reconceptualization of what is meant by economic growth since the very way economic indicators are currently measured "acts as a major contributor to environmental degradation."[17]

Belize is already exporting butterflies and butterfly pupae, an activity that could be expanded within a biosphere environment. And such forest-based economic development need not be limited to exports or to primary production. Southern Belize increasingly experiences a lack of sufficient bay palm fronds for housing thatch, forcing people to use the inferior cohune palm. By establishing private and public biospheres, the country could guarantee an adequate supply of bay palms and medicinal plants for domestic consumption. Extraction from forest biospheres could also be closely linked to secondary activities such as producing concentrates of forest fruits or medicinal plant extracts, thereby increasing the benefit to the local economy. The Rio Bravo Resource Management and Conservation Area sponsored by Program for Belize is based on this bioreserve concept.

Environmentally aware production does not necessarily lead to broad-based economic development, since control over resources and production could devolve to a privileged elite. For that reason, groups like the Institute for Economic Botany in New York propose that ecological impact studies be accompanied by socioeconomic impact studies that examine the social distribution of the benefits from biosphere reserves. Rather than resulting in the creation of new economic enclaves, the biosphere reserves would ideally promote community involvement and equitable distribution of income as beneficial byproducts of sustainable patterns of development.[18]

6

Foreign Influence

© Tony Villanueva

U.S. Foreign Policy

The United States has long been Belize's leading trading partner, and after independence this economic bond strengthened. At the same time, Washington moved to incorporate the country into its foreign policy strategy for Central America and the Caribbean. In the 1980s the United States came to exercise an influential role in just about every aspect of political, social, and economic life in Belize. This influence—both governmental and private—ranged from an influx of Peace Corps volunteers to a U.S. military/civic action project, from establishing the country's economic policies to restructuring its educational institutions. Since 1980 the U.S. trade surplus with Belize surged from $5 million to $26.5 million in 1990. While imports from the United States doubled during this period, exports to the United States rose only by $6 million.

By mid-decade Belize ranked as the second-largest per capita recipient of U.S. economic assistance (after El Salvador) in the Caribbean Basin. Its embassy staff had risen to 47, Peace Corps volunteers numbered more than 140, and a new Voice of America (VOA) transmitter was built in southern Belize. The increase in the official U.S. presence was paralleled by a flood of private U.S. organizations, churches, and businesses. With the embassy and the Agency for International Development (AID) leading the way, an array of evangelical missionaries, nongovernmental organizations (NGOs), and investors marched into this newly independent nation. At the same time Belize became saturated with U.S. television programming, pirated for the most part from satellite transmissions and rebroadcast into the living rooms of many Belizeans.

Washington, viewing Belize in strategic terms, has no single foreign policy objective for the country. At one point there was talk of establishing a military base in the country, but both Belize and the United States seem content with the present military arrangement with Britain. Belize has been regarded as easy pickings by Washington in its effort to shore up U.S. hegemony in the Caribbean Basin. With a minimal amount of money, the United States thus succeeded in tightening its hold on yet another country in the region. According to AID's 1986 Country Development Strategy Statement:

> Belize plays a strategic role as a stable, democratic bridge between the Caribbean and Central America regions. More importantly, it is poised on the edge of foment in Central America, where it serves as an important counterpoint to the unstable political and economic situations of its neighbors. . . . Belize also tends to look increasingly to the United States for economic and political support . . . the government firmly supports U.S. policies in the Caribbean and Central America.

As many will tell you, "Belizeans love Americans." One reason for this fondness is that many Belizeans are in fact U.S. residents. Some 55,000 to 65,000 Belizeans live in the United States, and their remittances to relatives back home constitute as much as one-quarter of the country's foreign exchange. Historically Belizeans often looked to the United States as a symbol of freedom in their country's fight for political independence. While other countries in Central America have long been accustomed to the neocolonial ways of the United States, Belizeans only received their first real taste in the 1980s. For the most part, though, the reaction was favorable. The increased U.S. presence has brought more money, jobs, and opportunities.

U.S. Trade and Investment

The United States is Belize's leading trading partner and prime source of foreign investment (Figure 6a). Its proximity to the Gulf Coast ports of New Orleans and Texas has facilitated this domination. Most British goods are, in fact, transshipped through New Orleans. Other favorable factors in the U.S.-Belize trade relationship are the U.S. sugar quota and the duty-free provisions of the Caribbean Basin Initiative (CBI).[1] During the 1980s the injection of U.S. economic assistance, stipulating that funds be used to purchase U.S. goods and services, magnified this U.S. trade orientation (Figure 6a).

Foreign investors have long played a commanding role in the Belizean economy. In the past, though, most of the major players have been British, including such large firms as Tate & Lyle and Barclays Bank. Throughout the last several decades individual U.S. investors have claimed a stake in the country's tourism and agricultural industries. Ramada Inns, which has a one-third investment in the new Ramada Royal Reef Hotel, is the leading brand name in the Belize tourist industry. There are also dozens of individual investors and smaller firms, perhaps the largest of which is Journey's End. Hershey is the most prominent name in U.S. agricultural investment in Belize, but it is joined by many other smaller investors in citrus, bananas, cattle, and nontraditional agroexports. Coca-Cola, which still holds 50,000 acres in northwest Belize, has no plans to develop that acreage for citrus in the immediate future.

Among the largest U.S. investors are Hershey Foods Corporation (cacao growing and processing), Chase Manhattan (interest in Atlantic Bank), Prosser Fertilizer, Ramada Inns, Texaco (petroleum distribution), Esso (petroleum distribution), Yalbac (citrus, timber, ranching), and Williamson Industries (assembling Dixie Jeans for export).[2]

In addition to Williamson Industries, which has a plant near Belize City, there is one other large U.S. apparel-assembly company as well as at least one Korean and two Chinese garment factories. Fyffes, a marketing affiliate of United Brands, buys most of the country's bananas. In the area of nontraditional agricultural production, a few fly-by-night U.S. investors were initially attracted by the subsidies offered through AID programs but have since left the country. Similarly, U.S. investments in the shrimp industry collapsed from insufficient capital and inexperience.

Tourism has been a bright spot on the economic scene, and a steady increase in the flow of U.S. visitors to the country has been one reason for this success. According to the U.S. Commerce Department, 45 percent of all tourists are U.S. citizens and Belize "has all the ingredients to become a popular U.S. tourist destination." In an effort to put the country on the jet-set map, AID has channeled development assistance funds into tourism and has encouraged the PUP government's new emphasis on ecotourism—signaling a change in PUP's former prohibition against subsidizing this economic sector. In a related development, plans are under way to attract U.S. retirees to Belize. To encourage this trend, the Belizean government has exempted

Figure 6a

U.S. Trade and Investment in Belize, 1990

In U.S. $.

U.S. share of Belize exports	51%
U.S. share of Belize imports	56%

Principal U.S. imports from Belize

Citrus concentrate, seafood, apparel, papaya, and wood.

Principal U.S. exports to Belize

General merchandise, petroleum products, capital equipment, motor vehicles, animal feed, and fertilizer.

Belize trade balance with United States	-$26.5 million

Top three U.S. investors

Esso, Hershey Foods, Williamson Industries.

Estimated U.S. investment	$50 million (55 firms)

SOURCE: U.S. Embassy, "Business Facts Sheets," March 1991; U.S. Embassy, "Investment Climate Statement," April 1990.

all foreign pension funds from the national income tax. In the private sector, a development company in Florida is exploring the possibility of establishing a retirement community in the country.

The recent emphasis on tourism marks a change in the Belizean government's own development priorities. Under the first postindependence Price administration, government leaders were reluctant to promote projects that would, as one former government official put it, "turn Belize into a nation of waiters." Although this remains a concern among many Belizeans, the dollars and jobs generated by the industry represent a welcome alternative to unemployment, economic stagnation, and outward migration.

The major issue facing the PUP government in its relations with Washington is free trade. Belize fears that U.S. free trade initiatives in Latin America and the Caribbean—notably the proposed North American Free Trade Agreement (NAFTA) and the Enterprise for the Americas Initiative—will undermine its place in the U.S. market, particularly for sugar and citrus but also for nontraditional exports. It is the position of both the government and private producers that Belize cannot compete against larger exporters such as Mexico and Brazil where productivity is higher and labor cheaper. Belize benefits from preferential access to the U.S. market under the Caribbean Basin Initiative and under the sugar import-quota program. Hemispheric free trade initiatives could severely curtail the country's exports to the United States by forcing the elimination of those programs. Nevertheless, Belize has entered into a framework agreement for trade liberalization negotiations together with the Caricom nations. Although fearing the advent of free trade, Belize wants a seat at the table in the hope that it can negotiate to retain its preferential access. Failing this, Belize at least wants to make certain that it is not left behind in the event that free trade does prevail.

U.S. Economic Aid

From 1981 to 1983 AID funds were distributed to Belize through the Caribbean regional office; but just two years after independence, an AID Mission was opened in Belize adjacent to the U.S. embassy. Discussions toward a significantly expanded AID program began during the PUP government, but not until the UDP's Esquivel became prime minister did large sums of U.S. economic assistance begin flowing into Belize. In terms of per capita U.S. aid, Belize quickly ranked among the world's top recipients. From 1980 through 1989 Belize received nearly $100 million in U.S. economic assistance.[3]

This large injection of aid was felt in most areas of society and the economy. Balance-of-payments support through AID's Economic Support Funds (ESF) allowed the country to meet its international obligations while maintaining an adequate reserve of foreign exchange. The local currency generated by the sale of ESF dollars was disbursed throughout the government's operating budget, providing the necessary funds for numerous public-works projects (particularly rural road construction), education and health programs, and investment and export-promotion schemes. Development assistance funds have gone to such projects as Livestock Development, Commercialization of Alternative Crops, Agricultural Marketing, Child Survival Support, Accelerated Cocoa Production, Export Investment Credit, and Employment Training.

To receive this aid, the Belizean government was obligated to fulfill certain conditions and adopt proposed policy reforms, particularly in the economic realm. Generally, AID insisted that the government liberalize its internal and external economy, utilizing government programs and funds to promote increased private investment and export production. AID stipulated, for example, that the government undertake a "comprehensive review of the foreign trade and import-licensing practices to determine a set of polices which will promote economically efficient productive investment." It obligated the government to remove all controls on domestic prices and foreign trade, and pressured the Esquivel administration to privatize parastatal corporations such as the Banana Control Board.

The UDP government, which wholeheartedly approved of AID's neoliberal development philosophy, fully complied with AID demands for policy changes and government restructuring. AID consultants were even assigned to various ministries to formulate the Belizean government's own development plans. The government's Food and Agricultural Policy Statement, for example, was largely the work of AID consultants and, not surprisingly, mirrored AID's own development priorities for Belize. As a result of AID's support and policy leverage, "many trade restrictions and price controls have been eliminated and major parastatals restructured or privatized."[4]

AID's reputation in Belize was damaged by a federal court conviction of the former head of the AID Mission, Neboysha Brashish, for improperly using his influence to obtain jobs and contracts for his wife and children. Also tarnishing the U.S. image in Belize was the 1988 revelation that the former U.S. ambassador to Belize, Malcolm Barnaby, had been involved in a major business transaction in the country. Soon after leaving his post, Barnaby became a consultant for a consortium that bought several hundred thousand acres in northeast Belize. The subsequent placement of a black woman, Mosina Jordan, to head the AID mission helped improve AID's image in Belize. Jordan, who describes herself as an "adviser to government," became recognized as a strong advocate of neoliberal policies and private-sector-led growth.[5]

Another U.S. public-relations embarrassment in Belize was the seemingly ubiquitous presence of Peace Corps volunteers. At one point, some 140 volunteers worked not only in community jobs but also in government offices in Belmopan, in the Chamber of Commerce, in the country's secondary schools, and as advisors for microenterprise projects throughout the country. Eventually, in response to Belizean concerns that the volunteers were taking away local jobs and unduly interfering in government ministerial matters, the Peace Corps contingent was reduced to 73 volunteers by 1991. The majority of these volunteers serve in education and youth development projects. The Peace Corps is now coordinating with the Ministry of Education to expand its environmental education initiative. Since its initial presence in Belize in 1962, the Peace Corps has placed over 1,300 volunteers.

Scholarship and training programs constitute another aspect of the U.S. economic aid program in Belize. Under the Central American Peace Scholarship Program (CAPS), over 300 Belizeans have received education in the United States. This augments regular

Figure 6b

U.S. Economic Aid to Belize, 1946-1992

In millions of U.S. $.

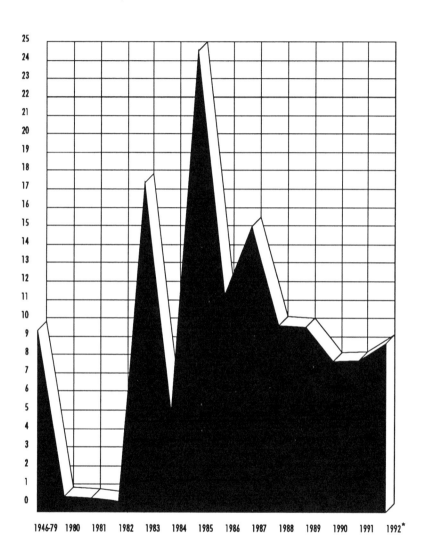

SOURCE: U.S. Overseas Loans and Grants: Obligations and Loan Authorizations, July 1, 1945-Sept. 30, 1983; July 1, 1945-Sept. 30, 1985; July 1, 1945-Sept. 30, 1987; July 1, 1945-Sept. 30, 1989; July 1, 1945-Sept. 30, 1991.
*Estimate.

training and exchange programs managed by the United States Information Agency (USIA). Economic aid also sponsored a program to send secondary and primary school administrators for training in the United States (see Schools and Education).

After an initial infusion of aid in 1983 and 1985, U.S. economic commitments to Belize fell to about $10 million by 1988. As earlier ESF grants were eliminated, AID's development assistance fell to $6.8 million (adding to $1.4 million for Peace Corps) by 1991 (Figure 6b). Budget constraints, competing demands for U.S. assistance, and diminished U.S. foreign policy concern for Central America were factors contributing to the lower assistance levels to Belize. With Belize having undertaken most of the financial restructuring and policy reforms advocated by Washington and the International Monetary Fund (IMF), AID's development assistance currently focuses on the tourism and agricultural sectors, with environmental protection, natural resources management, promotion of nontraditional agroexports, and improved rural roads among its major projects.

As elsewhere in the region, AID channels much of its aid through the private sector. Several new business organizations—including the National Development Foundation, Belize Export and Investment Promotion Unit, and Belize Institute for Management—were initially sustained entirely by AID grants. An array of U.S. and local nongovernmental organizations also emerged as a result of AID funding (see Nongovernmental Organizations).

Private-sector promotion and economic policy reform remain top U.S. priorities. In its Policy Agenda and Strategy 1991-1995, AID acknowledged that without ESF donations its influence is reduced. Yet it pledges to seek its goals through policy dialogue with the government and by leveraging the influence that its development assistance provides. For example, if Belize accedes to the Enterprise for the Americas Initiative, AID promises to reduce the country's $26.6 million debt to AID by allowing the country to pay the interest in Belizean dollars which will be placed in a local fund to support the Program for Belize and the jaguar reserve. AID continues to advocate the slashing of taxes on exports and imports—which together constitute about 60 percent of the government's revenue base—and their replacement mainly by consumption taxes. AID also argues that the government could reduce social service spending by privatizing many public-sector activities such as health care.

U.S. Military Aid

Since 1981 the Pentagon has demonstrated a growing interest in Belize. It has pursued this interest through direct military assistance, training programs, and civic-action and humanitarian assistance projects. These latter projects range from bridge-building by U.S. combat

Figure 6c

U.S. Military Aid to Belize, 1946-1992

In millions of U.S. $.

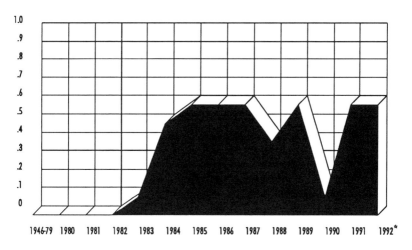

SOURCE: U.S. Overseas Loans and Grants: Obligations and Loan Authorizations, July 1, 1945-Sept. 30, 1983; July 1, 1945-Sept. 30, 1985; July 1, 1945-Sept. 30, 1987; July 1, 1945-Sept. 30, 1989; July 1, 1945-Sept. 30, 1991.
*Estimate.

engineer battalions to construction and repair work by Army Reserve and Air National Guard units at the Belize City Hospital and Price Barracks. In addition, U.S. military medical-training teams have on at least two occasions sponsored training exercises with the Belize Defense Force. According to the U.S. military attaché in Belize, such civic-action exercises are designed mainly to promote goodwill but they also serve to train U.S. army engineers in a tropical setting.[6]

Although the Pentagon recognizes Britain as Belize's main source of military aid, it has sought to complement that assistance and develop other avenues to strengthen the connections between the United States and the Belize Defense Force. From 1984 through 1989, Congress approved about a half million dollars' worth of military aid to Belize each year (Figure 6c). In 1990 U.S. military aid dropped to $100,000,[7] which according to the Department of Defense (DOD) "contributed to an erosion of Belizean confidence in the reliability of U.S. support." Congress bounced back in 1991 by approving credit financing of $500,000 in 1991 and 1992 in addition to the traditional $100,000 in annual International Military and Education Training (IMET) funding. About 20 BDF members are trained annually through the IMET program.[8] The Foreign Military Sales (FMS) credit-financing support is part of the U.S. government's program to bolster the BDF's capability to engage in counternarcotics operations.

There are five U.S. military personnel permanently stationed in Belize. A military liaison officer works directly with the Belize Defense Force while a U.S. military attaché advises the U.S. ambassador and the country's prime minister on defense matters. According to the DOD, "The United States seeks to sustain a democratic Belize, and to help it develop sufficient economic and military strength to maintain internal stability and combat a growing threat from Colombian narco-traffickers transshipping cocaine through Central America."[9] The U.S. government also provides equipment to the Serious Crime Unit that manages police antinarcotics operations.

Other Foreign Influences

Belize still celebrates the 1798 Battle of St. George's Caye, when residents, or Baymen, beat back a Spanish naval attack. That was the last time the Spanish tried to assert sovereignty over what came to be known as British Honduras. The territory was officially a British colony from 1862 to 1981. Although independent, Belize retains a strong British influence. From the educational system to the legal system, British structures remain largely intact.

The most obvious sign of British influence is, however, the some 1,500 British troops who remain in the country. Upon Belizean independence, the United Kingdom agreed to maintain a garrison in Belize to deter any aggression from Guatemala and to train the newly established Belize Defense Force. There is no set date for the British withdrawal, and most Belizeans are happy to see the troops stay in the country indefinitely. They are high-income consumers, so the departure of the British troops would severely impact the country's economic stability. One estimate attributed 15 percent of the country's GDP to the presence of the British garrison.[10] In 1991 Guatemala's recognition of Belize's independence raised the prospects of a British withdrawal within the next couple of years, although there were no announcements from London to that effect. Even if the troops themselves leave, it is likely that a small air force contingent will remain with several Harrier jets.

There have been concerns expressed in the British Parliament about the high cost of maintaining the troops in Belize (about 33 million British pounds annually). But a 1988 report by the Parliamentary Defense Committee projected a long stay for the British garrison. The committee noted that Belize is the last territory remaining where the British Defense Forces can train in challenging conditions. The tropical terrain makes training an "adventurous" undertaking. The committee also concluded that the troops addressed the "wider international concern" for having a well-trained foreign army in the region in addition to U.S. forces.[11]

Unstated, however, is the special relationship that the British garrison has to U.S. foreign policy. According to an analysis of British influence in Latin America by the Latin America Bureau in London, Washington favors the presence of the British garrison because it:

– Acts as a deterrent to leftist guerrillas who might use Belize as an arms conduit to Guatemala and El Salvador.

– Counters the accusation that the United States is the only external power in the region.

– Avoids the aggravation that U.S. military presence would create in U.S. relations with Guatemala.

– Averts increased Cuban influence in the region.[12]

Britain has long held second place after the United States in trade with Belize, and exports to the United Kingdom have been rising steadily since 1982. Following Britain, Belize's main trading partners are the Caricom nations (mainly Jamaica and Trinidad), other European Community nations, Mexico, and Canada (Figure 6d). Bilateral links with Britain are complemented by Belize's ties with the European Community (EC). Belize is one of the original Caribbean signatories of the Lomé Convention, a pact on trade, aid, and investment between the EC and more than 60 former European colonies. As a member of the Lomé Convention, Belize benefits from duty-free access to the EC market, preferential admittance of products that are part of the EC's Common Agricultural Policy, and inflated prices for sugar exports to the EC. Belizean producers are concerned that they

Figure 6d
Direction of Trade, January-June 1991

	% of total Exports	% of total Imports
United States	51.8	59.8
Britain ·	27.7	7.4
Other EC	1.6	7.6
Caricom	8.5	3.7
Mexico	2.7	9.1
Canada	7.0	2.4
Rest of World	0.7	10.0
	100.00	100.00

SOURCE: Office of Central Statistics (Belize City, Belize), February 1992.

will lose their preferential access to Europe as the European countries move toward the creation of a single undifferentiated market.

Most capital-account expenditures in Belize are covered by foreign assistance. One of the country's largest external creditors is the Caribbean Development Bank. Aside from financing large infrastructure projects, foreign development aid to Belize consists chiefly of grants for small-scale, community-based development in public health and agricultural production. Britain provided the loan, for example, to improve the Philip Goldson International Airport, including the lengthening of its runway to accommodate the large cargo planes used by British forces. The European Community is financing the improvement of the Hummingbird Highway and funds several human development projects. In 1991 Canada forgave $150 million in foreign debt while signing a new technical cooperation agreement with Belize. The Canadians have also facilitated increased manufactured imports from Belize and other Caribbean nations. Cuba sponsors a scholarship program for Belizean students and operates a health care program in Belize staffed by Cuban doctors and nurses. The government of Mexico is sponsoring the construction of a Mexico-Belize Cultural Institute in Belize City as well as establishing new trading and energy-distribution agreements with Belize. Belize also receives project aid from Canada, Venezuela, Taiwan, Germany, Japan, and South Korea.

Reference Notes

Introduction

1. Sir Eric S. Thompson, *Maya Archaeology* (Norman, OK: University of Oklahoma, 1971), pp. 71-2.
2. Local historian Leo Bradley quoted in D.G. Odaffer, "Three Capitals of British Honduras," thesis (San Francisco), 1970. Also see Richard Buhler's "What's in a Name?" *Brukdown*, Nos. 6-7, 1979.
3. Emory King, *I Spent It All in Belize* (Belize City: Tropical Books, 1986), p. 11. The flaw in this theory is that there is no firm historical evidence that pirate Peter Wallace ever visited what is now Belize.
4. David Hernández, "How Belize Got Its Name," Paper presented at Third Annual Studies on Belize Conference, October 26-28, 1989.
5. Central Statistical Office, "Provisional Results—1991 Census of Population and Housing" (Belmopan: March 1992). The 1991 census finds 194,300 Belizean citizens. Official government figures commonly underreport the refugee and immigrant population, which was at least 40,000 by 1991.
6. Robert Nicolait & Associates, *Belize: Country Environmental Profile* (Washington: Agency for International Development, 1984).
7. King, *I Spent It All in Belize*, p.11.
8. Grant D. Jones, *Maya Resistance to Spanish Rule: Time and History on a Colonial Frontier* (Albuquerque: University of New Mexico Press, 1989).
9. Preliminary 1991 census figures show the following urban concentration (in order of size): Belize 78 percent urban; Cayo 48 percent; Orange Walk 36 percent; Corozal 25 percent; Stann Creek 34 percent; and Toledo 19 percent.
10. See Lita Krohn, "State of Culture in Belize 1990," *Spear Reports* 7, 1990.

Part 1: Government and Politics

1. Upon leaving office the UDP, shocked by its defeat, lashed out against the PUP and the voters who had switched to the PUP, a sharp contrast with George Price's dignified transfer of power in 1984.
2. The 11 ministries are the following: Ministry of Finance, Home Affairs & Defense, and Trade & Commerce; Ministry of Industry and Natural Resources; Ministry of Foreign Affairs, Economic Development, and Education; Ministry of Energy and Communications; Ministry of Agriculture and Fisheries; Ministry of Housing and Cooperatives; Ministry of Social Services and Community Development; Attorney General's Ministry and Ministry of Tourism and the

Environment; Ministry of Health and Urban Development; Ministry of Works; and Ministry of Labor and Local Government & Social Services.

3. I.E. Sanchez, "Our Political Contract: Amendments and Additions," *Spear Reports* 7, 1990, pp. 64-70.

4. So strict is the secrecy of the Cabinet that if it can be proved that a minister has revealed its inner workings, he or she is liable to prosecution.

5. See Assad Shoman, *Party Politics in Belize: 1950-1986* (Belize: Cubola Productions, 1987), pp. 52-4, for a good description of Cabinet government in Belize.

6. This section on government structure is drawn from *How We Are Governed* (Belmopan: Government Information Service, 1990) and Shoman, *Party Politics*.

7. O. Nigel Bolland, *Belize: A New Nation in Central America* (Boulder: Westview Press, 1986), p. 105.

8. Ibid., p. 113.

9. Ibid., p. 109.

10. Quoted in Shoman, *Party Politics*, p. 62. Price's specific model for the PUP was the British Labor Party.

11. Ibid., p. 63. Shoman further argues on p. 89 that a real process of decolonization in Belize never took place because the political parties, controlled as they were by middle-class leaders, chose to maintain the prevailing economic and social structures of the colony and effectively prevented mass participation in political decisionmaking.

12. Ibid., p. 59.

13. For a history of political parties see: C.H. Grant, *The Making of Modern Belize* (Cambridge: Cambridge University Press, 1976) and Shoman, *Party Politics*.

14. *Central America Report*, September 8, 1989; *Belize Briefing*, August 1989.

15. Dean Barrow, "A UDP Response to the Budget," *Spearhead*, April 1990.

16. See Beth Sims, *National Endowment for Democracy (NED): A Foreign Policy Branch Gone Awry* (Albuquerque: Resource Center, 1990).

17. Assad Shoman, "Belize: A Democratic Authoritarian State," Paper presented to the Second Annual Studies on Belize Conference (Belize City), October 1988.

18. Gordon Lewis called *personalismo* a characteristic feature of political parties in the Caribbean, defining this quality as "the intimate bond that unites charismatic leaders and adulatory followers in a form of political messianism." Gordon K. Lewis, *Growth of the Modern West Indies* (London: McGibbon & Kee, 1968), p. 229.

19. Shoman, *Party Politics*, p. 63.

20. "The Democratic Direction of the People's United Party" (Belize City, mimeo, 1982).

21. *Belize Briefing*, August 1989.

22. C.H. Grant in his authoritative book on colonial Belize observed, "The PUP has never wavered in its belief that heavy foreign capital investment is a prerequisite for economic growth. Furthermore, PUP policy continues to favor the exploitation of the country's natural resources by corporate American capital." Grant, *The Making of Modern Belize*, p. 229. Bolland described the PUP's ideology as "antisocialist as well as anticolonial and pro-free enterprise as well as pro-American." Bolland, *Belize: A New Nation*, p. 113.

23. Government of Belize, *Development Plan 1990-1994* (Belmopan, 1990), p. 1.

24. Historically, the PUP's leftists were Said Musa and Assad Shoman, two British-educated lawyers who have been dedicated to a progressive social and economic vision of Belize since the 1960s. Both served as ministers in the 1979-84 PUP government and continually fended off redbaiting attacks. After the 1984 elections, Shoman left the party to do grassroots education through SPEAR (Society for the Promotion of Education and Research) while Musa became party chairperson.

25. *Belize Briefing*, September 1989. Florencio Marin, the leader of the opposition from 1984 to 1989, lost his seat in the House of Representatives and was appointed by Price to be deputy prime minister. Said Musa won an easy victory over Dean Lindo and was appointed to head the ministries of Foreign Affairs, Economic Development, and Education.

26. "Belizeans First with the People's United Party 1989-1994," party manifesto; interview with Said Musa in *Spearhead*, September 1989; *Central America Report*, September 8, 1989.

27. Roberto Bardini, *Belize: Historia de una Nacion en Movimiento* (Tegucigalpa: Editorial Universitaria, 1978), p. 172.

28. "Prime Minister's Address to the Nation," January 17, 1984.
29. The United States, particularly through the Agency for International Development (AID), took an active role in shaping the country's economic policy in the 1980s. According to Shoman, "The United States intervened in domestic political affairs and actively aided in the electoral defeat of the PUP which, for all its protestations about the United States being a natural ally, was not then itself regarded by the United States as a sufficiently compliant and reliable one." Assad Shoman, "Belize: From Colony to Independent State," Paper prepared for the XVI Annual Conference of the Caribbean Studies Association (La Habana, Cuba), May 21-24, 1991, p. 22.
30. Cedric Grant, "Belize: Multiple External Orientation: The Caribbean Dimension," Paper presented at the 12th International Congress of the Caribbean Studies Association (Belize City), May 1987, pp. 4-5.
31. Belize Government Information Service, "The New Belize," June 1985.
32. Carla Barnett and Assad Shoman, "Belize in Central America and the Caribbean: Peace, Development, and Integration," Paper prepared for a conference in Belize, June 24-26, 1988.
33. Julio A. Fernandez, *Belize: Case Study for Democracy in Central America* (Aldershot, England: Avebury, 1989), p. 80.
34. The following chronology of the Anglo-Guatemalan dispute is drawn largely from Shoman, "From Colony to Independent State."
35. Bardini, *Belize: Historia de una Nacion*, which detailed the planned invasion, was the first book published in Spanish about Belize and greatly aided the government's efforts to gain Latin American, particularly Central American, support for independence.
36. Bolland, *Belize: A New Nation*, p. 135.
37. Ministry of Economic Development, Central Statistical Office, Abstract of Statistics (Belmopan: November 1990). These percentages are taken from the 1988 fiscal year.
38. "The Belize Defense Force Now Ten Years Old," *Belize Today*, January 1988; interview by Debra Preusch with Bill Tillet, then permanent secretary in the Ministry of Defense, March 19, 1987.
39. "BDF Prepares to Fight Narco-Guerrillas," *Belize Today*, August 1991.
40. Lawyers Committee for Human Rights, *Critique: Review of the Department of State's Country Reports on Human Rights Practices for 1989* (New York: 1990).
41. Lawyers Committee for Human Rights, *Critique: Review of the Department of State's Country Reports on Human Rights Practices for 1990* (New York: July 1991).
42. *Mesoamérica*, December 1988.
43. Interview with Billy Heusner, January 7, 1992.
44. Interview with Billy Heusner, March 8, 1990.
45. Human Rights Commission of Belize, "Report: Belize City Prison," 1991.
46. Interview with Billy Heusner, January 7, 1992.

Part 2: Economy

1. For a review and analysis of the economy in the 1980s see: World Bank, *Belize Economic Memorandum* (Washington: December 1989).
2. This government spending spree helps explain the record $96 million budget deficit in 1989.
3. U.S. Embassy, "Economic Trends: Belize" (Belize City), December 1990; Midwest Universities Consortium for International Activities, *An Assessment of Belize's Agricultural Sector* (Belize City: AID and Ministry of Agriculture, March 1988).
4. Of the total external public debt registered by September 1991, roughly 44 percent was owed to bilateral sources, 42 percent to multilateral sources, 15 percent to commercial banks, and 1 percent to suppliers. Central Bank of Belize, *Quarterly Review*, December 1991.
5. See AID, *Policy Agenda and Strategy 1991-1995* (Belize City: August 31, 1989). One of the main priorities of AID in Belize is to push for a tax reform that would remove the tax burden on trade and shift it mainly to direct consumption and user fees.

6. Joseph Perry, Louis Woods, and Jeffrey Steagall, "1992 and Beyond: Trade Policy Problems Facing Belize in a Changing World Market," Paper prepared for the Fifth Annual Studies on Belize Conference (Belize City), September 3-6, 1991, p. 4.

7. Official net international reserves climbed from $14 million in 1986 to $80 million in 1990.

8. *1990-1994 Development Plan*, p. 19. The IMF projected a decline in the terms of trade of approximately 11 percent between 1989 and 1994 as the average unit value of exports stagnates while that of imports rises due to inflation in industrialized countries.

9. Said Musa, "Statement to the General Assembly of the Organization of American States, January 8, 1991" (Belmopan: Government Printery, 1991), p. 2.

10. United Nations Development Program, *Human Development* (New York: 1991).

11. Dylan Vernon, "Belize: The First Decade of Independence in a Region of Crisis," Report prepared for FLACSO (Costa Rica), July 1990.

12. "Thick sediments, high potential postulated in Belize license area," *Oil & Gas Journal*, January 7, 1991, p. 87.

13. Cited in Louis Woods, Joseph Perry, and Jeffery Steagall, "International Tourism and Economic Development: Belize Ten Years After Independence," Paper prepared for the Fifth Annual Studies on Belize Conference (Belize City), September 3-6, 1991, p. 9.

14. A. Joy Grant, "The State of Belize's Environment: Towards Sustainable Development," Paper prepared for the Fifth Annual Studies on Belize Conference (Belize City), September 3-6, 1991.

15. Caribbean Tourism Research and Development Center, *Tourism Action Plan for Belize*, November 1985.

16. *Chamber Update*, July/August 1991, p. 3.

17. National Narcotics Intelligence Committee, "The NNICC Report 1989," June 1990, p. 53.

18. U.S. Department of Defense, *Congressional Presentation for Security Assistance Programs, FY1992* (Washington: 1991), p. 94.

19. Perry et al., "1992 and Beyond." See also Peta M. Henderson, "Development and Dependency in a Belizean Village," *Spear Reports*, No. 4, 1990.

20. Joseph M. Perry and Louis A. Woods, "Changing Agricultural Patterns in Belize since 1958," *Spear Reports*, No. 7, 1991, p. 89.

21. Mark Moberg, "Citrus and the State: Factions and Class Formation in Rural Belize," *American Ethnologist* 18, No. 2, May 1991, p. 217.

22. Mark Moberg, "Class Resistance and Class Hegemony: From Conflict to Co-optation in the Citrus Industry of Belize," *Ethnology* 29, No. 3, 1990, p. 193.

23. Two excellent overviews of class and ethnic tensions in the citrus industry are found in Moberg, "Class Resistance and Class Hegemony," and Laurie Kroshus-Medina, "Immigration, Labor and Government Policy: Class Conflict and Alternative Paths to Development," Paper prepared for the Fifth Annual Studies on Belize Conference (Belize City), September 3-6, 1991.

24. Moberg in "Class Resistance and Class Hegemony" offers a revealing look at ethnic conflicts within the United General Workers Union (UGWU) and the way that Garifuna leadership has blocked majority control by the Spanish-speaking members. According to Moberg, "The creation of a high-income sector within the citrus labor force has resulted in a 'segmented labor market,' rendering the union and citrus workers as a whole more malleable from the processors' point of view," p. 199.

25. Midwest Universities Consortium, *An Assessment*.

26. Emory King, "Editor's Notebook," *Belize Currents*, April-May 1989.

27. Nicolait & Associates, *Environmental Profile*, p. 83.

28. Midwest Universities Consortium, *An Assessment*.

29. Perry and Woods, "Changing Agricultural Patterns," p. 92.

30. For an excellent examination of this problem see: Mark Moberg, "Marketing Policy and the Loss of Food Self-Sufficiency in Rural Belize," *Human Organization* 50, No. 1, 1991.

Part 3: Society and Ethnicity

1. A thorough overview of the ethnic origins of Belizean society is found in O. Nigel Bolland, *Colonialism and Resistance in Belize: Essays in Historical Sociology* (Belize: Cubola Productions, 1988).
2. Meb Cutlack, "Belize as a World Heritage Site," *The Belize Review*, November 1991.
3. Bolland, *Colonialism and Resistance in Belize*, p. 200.
4. Narda Dobson, *A History of Belize* (London; Longman, 1973), pp. 243-58. Also see Paul Martin, "The Mennonites of Belize," *Belizean Studies* 1, No. 3, May 1973.
5. Jim Adair, "Belize Mennonites," *Belize Currents*, Summer 1990.
6. Grant, *The Making of Modern Belize*, p. 14.
7. For a more thorough discussion of what it means to be creole in Belize see Karen Judd, "Who Will Define Us? Creolization in Belize," *Spear Reports*, No. 4, Second Annual Studies on Belize Conference (Belize City), 1990.
8. *Profile of Belize* (Belize City: SPEAR, 1990), p. 9.
9. Evan X Hyde, *The Crowd Called UBAD* (Belize: Modern Printers, 1970), p. 10.
10. Cited in Trevor Munroe, *The Politics of Constitutional Decolonization: Jamaica 1944-1962* (Jamaica: Institute of Social and Economic Research, 1972).
11. Judd, "Who Will Define Us?" p. 37.
12. Peter David Ashdown, *Garveyism in Belize* (Belize: SPEAR, 1990).
13. See: Hyde, *The Crowd Called UBAD*, and Ismail Omar Shabazz, "The UBAD Experience and Legacy," Paper prepared for the Fifth Annual Studies on Belize Conference (Belize City), September 3-6, 1991.
14. See Horace Campbell, *Rasta and Resistance: From Marcus Garvey to Walter Rodney* (Trenton, New Jersey: Africa World Press, 1987).
15. Mervin Lambey, "Youths in Woolen Hats: Rastafari in Belize since 1980," Paper prepared for the Fifth Annual Studies on Belize Conference (Belize City), September 3-6, 1991. This paper, one of the only studies to examine Rastafarianism in Belize, places the Rasta culture in the context of the black consciousness movement, stating that the struggle is not over in Belize and that the need remains for "the elevation of the African people and culture to its rightful place among the peoples and the nations of the world."
16. Joseph O. Palacio, *Socioeconomic Integration of Central American Immigrants in Belize* (Belize: SPEAR, 1990), p. 14. Palacio states that many upwardly mobile *mestizos* downplay their Hispanic background while adopting the "mainstream Belize City disposition . . . trading in their 'Spanishness' and that of their children for acceptance into their social class setting."
17. Ibid., pp. 11-12.
18. Bolland, *Colonialism and Resistance in Belize*, p. 201.
19. Ibid., p. 203.
20. Marc Chapin and Richard Wilk, *Ethnic Minorities in Belize: Mopan, Kekchí, and Garifuna* (Belize City: SPEAR, 1990), p. 24.
21. Phrase used by Douglas Taylor, *The Black Caribs of British Honduras* (New York: Viking Fund Publications in Anthropology, 1951), p. 138.
22. Chapin and Wilk, *Ethnic Minorities in Belize*, p. 5.
23. See the works of James Gregory, including "The Mopan: Culture and Ethnicity in a Changing Belizean Community," Museum of Anthropology, University of Missouri, 1987, and "Pioneers on a Cultural Frontier: The Mopan Maya of British Honduras," University Microfilms, Ann Arbor, Michigan, 1972.
24. Chapin and Wilk, *Ethnic Minorities in Belize*, p. 18
25. Ibid.
26. Richard R. Wilk, "Mayan Ethnicity in Belize," *Cultural Survival Quarterly*, Vol. 10, No. 2, 1986, pp. 73-6.
27. Ibid.
28. Sebastian Cayetano, "The Maya/Kekchí of Belize: Some Teaching Notes," July 1986.
29. *Spearhead*, February-March 1987.
30. Gary Hartshorn et al., *Belize Country Environmental Profile: A Field Study* (San Jose: AID and Trejos Hnos., 1984), p. 21.

31. Ronald Wright, *Time Among the Maya* (New York: Weindenfeld & Nicholson, 1989).
32. Wilk, "Mayan Ethnicity in Belize," p. 73.
33. Byron Foster, ed., *Warlords and Maize Men* (Belize: Cubola Productions, 1989), p. 4.
34. Ibid., p. 32.
35. Nadine Epstein, "From a Remote Jungle Site a Trail of Striking Clues," *Belize Currents*, Spring 1990.
36. Mary DeLand Pohl, "The Rio Hondo Project in Northern Belize," in Mary DeLand Pohl, ed., *Ancient Maya Wetland Agriculture: Excavations on Albion Island, Northern Belize* (Boulder: Westview Press, 1990), pp. 1-19.
37. Eric S. Thompson, *The Maya of Belize: Historical Chapters Since Columbus* (Belize: Cubola Productions, 1988), pp. 5-6.
38. Information on the Mayan centers listed comes largely from Foster, *Warlords and Maize Men*.
39. Information taken largely from David M. Pendergast and Elizabeth Graham, "Life in an Ancient Ambergris Caye Town: The Marco Gonzalez Site," *Belize Currents*, Summer 1990.
40. Jaime J. Awe and Mark D. Campbell, *Cahal Pech—Cayo, Belize: A Preliminary Guide to the Ancient Ruins* (Belize City: Belize Tourism Industry Association, 1989).
41. See Epstein, "From a Remote Jungle Site."

Part 4: Social Forces and Institutions

1. This section on history is largely drawn from Byron Foster, *The Baymen's Legacy: A Portrait of Belize City* (Belize: Cubola Productions, 1987).
2. Shoman, *Party Politics*.
3. Joseph Palacio, "What Rural People are Saying about Rural Development," Paper prepared for the Fifth Annual Studies on Belize Conference (Belize City), September 3-6, 1991.
4. *Development Plan 1990-1994*, p. 9.
5. For more information about the Northern Fishermen's Cooperative, see: Glenn Godfrey, *Ambergris Caye: Paradise with a Past* (Belize: Cubola Productions, 1983); and Susanna Vega, "The Development of the Spiny Lobster in Belize, 1920-1977," *Belizean Studies*, Vol. 7, No. 2, 1979. Other economically sound fishermen's cooperatives are the Caribeña and National cooperatives.
6. See Moberg, "Marketing Policy and the Loss of Food Self-Sufficiency."
7. Moberg, "Citrus and the State," p. 223.
8. Quoted in Ibid., p. 222. Moberg argues that factionalism "has become an accepted feature of community life" because of the "intrusion of national party politics, which polarize kin and neighbor alike." Comparing two villages in Stann Creek, Moberg found that the more isolated and less populated village was "virtually overlooked by nonlocal politicians and is comparatively free of factional conflict."
9. The Ministry of Labor using 1984 data estimates 14 percent unemployment while the U.S. Embassy ("Business Facts Sheets," March 1991) puts the figure at 15 percent.
10. Ministry of Economic Development, Central Statistical Office, *Abstract of Statistics* (Belmopan, November 1990). Age of population based on 1989 projections.
11. *Development Plan 1990-1994*, p. 7.
12. Cited in Laurie Kroshus-Medina, "Immigration, Labor, and Government Policy: Class Conflict and Alternative Paths Towards Development," Paper prepared for the Fifth Annual Studies on Belize Conference (Belize City), September 3-6, 1991.
13. For more information on the history of unions in Belize, see: William L. Cumiford, "Belize," in Gerald Greenfield and Sheldon Maram, eds., *Latin American Labor Organizations* (Westport: Greenwood Press, 1987); O. Nigel Bolland, "The Labour Movement and the Genesis of Modern Politics in Belize," in Malcolm and Gad Heuman, eds., *Labour in the Caribbean: From Emancipation to Independence*, reproduced in Bolland, *Colonialism and Resistance in Belize*; Shoman, *Party Politics*; and Bolland, *Belize: A New Nation*.
14. See: Assad Shoman, "Double Jeopardy: Trade Union Relations with Party and State: The Case of the UGWU," Paper presented at the First Annual Studies on Belize Conference, June

1987, published in *Ethnicity and Development* (Belize City: SPEAR, 1987); and Laurie Kroshus-Medina, "Creating and Manipulating Power with Dependency," *Belizean Studies*, Vol. 16, No. 3, 1988.

15. Lawyers Committee, *Reports on Human Rights Practices for 1989.*
16. Ibid.
17. For an overview of the country's educational system, see: C.N. Young, "The Educational System of Belize," unpublished report, 1988.
18. Cynthia Thompson, "Pre-School and Primary Education in Belize," in *Education in Belize: Toward the Year 2000* (Belize: SPEAR, 1991), p. 31.
19. Assad Shoman, "Why a National Education Symposium?" in *Education in Belize: Toward the Year 2000* (Belize: SPEAR, 1991), citing World Bank, "Belize: Education Sector Review Report," January 1989, p. 6.
20. UNICEF, *Country Program Position Paper, UNICEF-Belize 1992-1996* (Belize City: March 1991), p. 2.
21. Central America Peace Scholarship Program/PIER Workshop Report, *The Admission and Placement of Students from Central America* (Washington: National Association of Foreign Student Affairs, 1987).
22. J. Alexander Bennett, "Higher Education in Belize: Aspirations, Frustrations, and New Directions," in *Spear Reports*, No. 6: Third Annual Studies on Belize Conference (Belize: SPEAR, 1990), pp. 6-16.
23. Describing the dismantling of BELCAST and the agreement with Ferris State, O. Nigel Bolland wrote, "The whole circumstance in which UCB is being established and the terms of the agreement between Belize and Ferris State College indicate that Belize's highest institution of education may be little more than a branch plant of the U.S. education system." O. Nigel Bolland, "United States Cultural Influences on Belize: Television and Education as 'Vehicles of Import,' " *Caribbean Quarterly*, September-December 1987. The agreement signed between the government and the Board of Control of Ferris State University ceded to the Board the right to establish UCB's academic program and to establish admission standards. The agreement stipulated that "the Government of Belize hereby waives any sovereign privileges and immunities" relative to possible disputes over the agreement and that such disputes would be submitted to the jurisdiction of the Michigan Court of Claims.
24. Pre-election interview by Diane Haylock with Said Musa, *Spearhead*, September 1989, p. 9.
25. "Minister Musa Calls for Education to Empower Belizeans," *Spearhead*, December 1990.
26. Barrow, "A UDP Response."
27. SPEAR Press Release, March 5, 1990.
28. Belize Government Information Services/Pan American Health Organization, "Priority Health Needs," November 1985.
29. Ministry of Health, *National Health Planning System 1990-1994* (Belize City: PAHO-WHO, November 1990).
30. Government Information Services, "Priority Health Needs."
31. UNICEF, *Program Position, 1992-1996*, p. 1.
32. Interview by Debra Preusch with Dr. César Hermida of Pan American Health Organization/Belize, May 2, 1989.
33. Figures from the 1980 Belize Census show the following percentage breakdown of religious preference: Roman Catholic, 61.7 percent; Anglican, 11.8 percent; Methodist, 6 percent; Mennonite, 3.9 percent; Seventh Day Adventist, 3 percent; Pentecostal, 2.2 percent; Nazarene, 1.1 percent; Jehovah's Witnesses, 1 percent; Baptist, 0.9 percent; and others/not stated, 8.4 percent.
34. *Spearhead*, March-April 1988.
35. The important contributions of Belizean women in forming early organizations of nurses, teachers, and other groups are recognized in Silvana Woods, *Mothers of Modern Belize* (Belize: National Women's Commission, 1991), a book that charts the lives of four Belizean woman.
36. See *Notable Women in Belize* (Belize: Women Against Violence, c1990), which highlights portraits of the 19 women who have received the Women's Liberation Award.
37. Lawyers Committee, *Reports on Human Rights Practices for 1990*, p. 31.
38. Cited in Ibid., p. 28.

39. Ibid., p. 29.
40. "The Strategy for Integration of Refugees of the Government of Belize," Presented at the International Conference on Central American Refugees (Belize City), January 20, 1992.
41. Joseph O. Palacio, "A Rural/Urban Environment for Central American Immigrants in Belize," *Caribbean Quarterly*, September-December 1987.
42. Palacio, *Socioeconomic Integration of Central American Immigrants*, p. 23.
43. Immigration Advisory Committee Final Report; Cabinet Memo No. 40 of 1987.
44. "The Strategy for Integration of Refugees of the Government of Belize," Presented at the International Conference on Central American Refugees (Belize City), January 20, 1992.
45. Palacio, *Socioeconomic Integration of Central American Immigrants*, pp. 11, 13. Palacio states that an "anti-Central American ideology" is prevalent in Belize and is most commonly found in Belize City "where it feeds on itself through constant elaboration in the mass media gradually assuming the characteristics of an accepted fact." The guardians of this ideology include "the leaders of government, the church, private sector, and NGOs. The mechanisms they use to perpetuate it are the mass media."
46. The U.S. Embassy estimates the Belizean population in the United States to be 50,000, but this appears to be an underestimate according to Dylan Vernon, "Belizean Exodus to the United States: For Better or For Worse," Paper presented at the Second Annual Studies on Belize Conference (Belize City), 1988.
47. See, for example, Leslie Snyder, Connie Roser, and Steven Chaffee, "Foreign Media and the Desire to Emigrate from Belize," *Journal of Communication* 41, No. 1, Winter 1991. The authors point out that the foreign media bring mixed messages to Belize, news of crime, racial hatred, and violence as well as of consumer wealth, and they suggest that interpersonal networks may be a more powerful source of motivations to emigrate.
48. "Belizean Exodus: Dominance of the Creole," *Spearhead*, March 1989.

Part 5: The Environment

1. H. Leonard Jeffrey, *Natural Resources and Economic Development in Central America* (New Brunswick: Transaction Books, 1987); Georgia Tasker, "Some Wins, Some Losses," *Miami Herald*, October 9, 1988.
2. Regulated but nonprotected forest reserves include Swazey Bladen, Machaca, Deep River, Silk Grass, Maya Mountain, Freshwater Creek, Mt. Pine Ridge, Grants Work, Sibun, Mango Creek, Columbia River, Commerce Bight, and Sittee. Special Development Areas are largely protected but limited *milpa* cultivation, hunting, and other economic activities are still permitted.
3. Midwest Universities Consortium, *An Assessment*, p. 13, citing data from Lands and Surveys Records, Ministry of Natural Resources, October 1984.
4. Grant, "The State of Belize's Environment."
5. Apt Associates, *Belize Natural Resource Policy Inventory* (Washington: AID/ROCAP, October 1990), p. 28. The account of problems in land use and water quality comes largely from this survey.
6. J.S. Perkins, *The Belize Barrier Reef Ecosystem: An Assessment of its Resources, Conservation Status, and Management* (The New York Zoological Society and the Yale School of Forestry and Environmental Studies, 1983); R.D. Glaholt, *Belize Spiny Lobster Stock Assessment and Management Plan* (Canadian International Development Agency, 1986).
7. Janet Gibson and Vincent Gillet, "Recreation Pollution: A Major Problem," *Belize Review*, August 1991.
8. These include Half Moon Caye, Crooked Tree, Cockscomb, Guanacaste, Blue Hole, Bladen, Five Blue Lakes, and Society Hall and a working relationship with the Community Baboon Sanctuary.
9. Peter Furley, ed., *Advances in Environmental and Biogeographical Research in Belize* (University of Edinburgh, 1989), pp. 70-79.
10. Dr. Alan Rabinowitz, Wildlife Conservation International, "Belize Trip Report," June 1-July 30, 1991.

11. *Scientific American*, May 1991, p. 32.

12. Clara Germani, "How a Zoo Helps Save Belize," *Christian Science Monitor*, June 17, 1991.

13. Steele Wotkyns, "Conserving the Bladen Rainforest," *Earth Island Journal*, Summer 1988.

14. F. Lewis Cavanaugh, "Save the Rainforest: A Program for Belize," *Belize Currents*, Vol. 1, No. 1, 1989.

15. These were BAS President James Waight, Vice-President Margaret Craig, and Secretary Lydia Waight.

16. This history of the relationship between the Belize and Massachusetts Audubon Societies is taken largely from Michael Mitchell, "International Assistance and Organization Development: Constraints on Nature Conservation in Belize," Thesis for Master of Science (University of Tennessee, Knoxville), December 1990.

17. Grant, "The State of Belize's Environment."

18. Robert M. Heinzman and Conrad Reinign, "Report on Non-Timber Forest Products in Belize and their Role in Biosphere Reserve Modes" (New York: Institute for Economic Botany, 1990).

Part 6: Foreign Influence

1. As a CBI beneficiary, Belize enjoys duty-free entry of all items exported to the United States, with the exception of textiles and apparel (which are subject to the Multifiber Agreement), canned tuna, petroleum, footwear, and certain leather products.

2. U.S. Embassy, "Investment Climate Statement: Belize," March 1989.

3. U.S. Agency for International Development, *Congressional Presentation, FY1990, Annex III* (Washington, 1989).

4. U.S. Agency for International Development, *Congressional Presentation, FY1992* (Washington, 1991), p. 720.

5. "Interview with USAID's Mosina Jordan," *Chamber Update*, April 1991.

6. Ibid.

7. Agency for International Development, *U.S. Overseas Loans and Grants: Obligations and Loan Authorizations, July 1, 1945-September 30, 1990* (Washington, 1990).

8. U.S. Department of Defense, *Congressional Presentation for Security Assistance Programs, FY 1992* (Washington, 1991).

9. Ibid.

10. Anthony J. Payne, "The Belize Triangle: Relations with Britain, Guatemala, and the United States," *Journal of InterAmerican Studies and World Affairs* 32, No. 1, Spring 1990, p. 123.

11. *Belize Briefing*, January 1989.

12. *The Thatcher Years: Britain and Latin America* (London: Latin America Bureau, 1988).

Selected Bibliography

History and Politics

O. Nigel Bolland, *Colonialism and Resistance in Belize: Essays in Historical Sociology* (Belize: Cubola Productions, 1988).

O. Nigel Bolland, *Belize: A New Nation in Central America* (Boulder: Westview Press, 1986).

Assad Shoman, *Party Politics in Belize: 1950-1986* (Belize: Cubola Productions, 1987).

C.H. Grant, *The Making of Modern Belize* (Cambridge: Cambridge University Press, 1976).

Byron Foster, *The Baymen's Legacy: A Portrait of Belize City* (Belize: Cubola Productions, 1987).

Society for the Promotion of Education and Research, *Spear Reports* (Belize City: 1989-91).

Culture and Travel

Ronald Wright, *Time Among the Maya* (New York: Weindenfeld & Nicholson, 1989).

Byron Foster, ed., *Warlords and Maize Men* (Belize: Cubola Productions, 1989).

Chicki Mallan, *Belize Handbook* (Chico, CA: Moon Publications, 1991).

Paul Glassman, *Belize Guide* (Champlain: Passport Press, 1990).

Richard Mahler and Steele Wotkyns, *Belize: A Natural Destination* (Santa Fe: John Muir Press, 1991).

Chronology

1763   Treaty of Paris signed allowing the British to cut wood and export logwood, but asserting Spanish sovereignty over the country.

1779   The Spanish attack British settlers for the fourth time since 1717.

1783   Treaty of Versailles signed with terms similar to Treaty of Paris.

1786   Convention of London signed allowing Baymen to cut wood but not establish plantations, fortifications, or government in Belize territory; first British superintendent to Belize.

1798   British defeat Spanish in the Battle of St. George's Caye.

1816   Spain protests erection of fortification in Belize.

1817   British superintendent assumes authority to grant land titles.

1820   Fourth recorded slave revolt since 1765.

1821   Central American region declares its independence from Spain.

1823   U.S. pronouncement of the Monroe Doctrine.

1824   There are an estimated 2,300 slaves in Belize, including Africans, creoles, and descendants of Indians.

1831   "Coloured subjects of free condition" are granted civil rights.

1838   Emancipation (four years after Britain) of slaves, who compose less than one-half of the population. Free blacks and coloreds compose about half the population, and whites about one-tenth.

1839   Central American federation disintegrates; Guatemala claims to have inherited sovereign rights over Belize from Spain.

1840   Laws of England declared to be in force in Belize; Executive Council formed to assist superintendent. Spain does not attempt to reassert its authority.

1850   U.S.-British treaty; Britain agrees to refrain from occupying, fortifying, or colonizing any part of Central America. Britain claims that this treaty exempts Belize as a prior settlement.

1854   Formal constitution adopted, providing for Legislative Assembly. Belize is now "a colony in all but name."

1855   Legal system regularized.

1859	Guatemala recognizes British sovereignty but claims that it signed the treaty because Britain agreed to build a road to the Caribbean coast.
1862	Officially declared a colony and recognized as part of the British Commonwealth with the name British Honduras.
1863	Treaty with Guatemala which further defines the road-building responsibilities.
1871	Status changed to crown colony under governor in Jamaica; Legislative Council with five official and four unofficial members.
1884	Colonial ties to Jamaica severed; separate colony status announced.
	Guatemala threatens to repudiate treaty of 1859.
1890	A request is made to introduce elected members. Request turned down because in a population of 30,000, only 400 are white.
1893	Treaty with Mexico settling a boundary dispute.
1894	Mahogany workers organize.
1919	Belizean soldiers returning from World War I protest discrimination in Ex-Servicemen's Riot.
1922	Establishment of the Civil Service Association.
1931	Hurricane hits the country; Britain supplies aid for reconstruction and regains reserve powers under new constitution.
1936	Constitution promulgated with elective principle. Property, income, and literacy qualifications restrict eligible voters.
	Britain offers 50,000 pounds to help build the road to the coast without admitting liability; Guatemala demands 400,000 pounds.
1937	Formation of the Laborers and Unemployed Association (LUA), which stages boycotts and demonstrations.
1939	Formation of the British Honduras Workers and Tradesmen Union, which later becomes the General Workers Union (1943).
1941	Mass meetings held; demands made for adult suffrage and the right to elect the government.
	Labor unions legalized by colonial governor.
1945	"Belice" is defined as the 23rd department in Guatemala's new constitution.
1949	People's Committee formed to protest devaluation of British Honduras dollar.
1950	Formation of People's United Party (PUP).
	Minimum age for women voters lowered from 30 to 21.
1952	General Workers Union (GWU) mounts 49-day strike.
1954	New constitution promulgated which provides for universal adult suffrage, and elected majority in Legislative Council.
	PUP begins 30-year winning streak in all general and most local elections.
1955	Semi-ministerial government introduced but governor keeps reserve powers.

1958	Formation of National Independence Party (NIP) as first political opposition to PUP.
1960	In a new constitution, a majority of the Executive Council is elected.
1961	Belize obtains associate-member status in the United Nations Economic Commission for Latin America.
	Belize turns down offer to become an "associate state" of Guatemala.
	Hurricane Hattie levels Belize City.
1962	Formation of National Federation of Christian Trade Unions.
1963	Guatemala breaks off negotiations with Britain, threatens war.
1964	In movement toward independence, the Executive Council of the governor evolves from an advisory council to a Cabinet of ministers, and reserve powers are practically eliminated.
	Control of local government passes to Belize, with Britain retaining control over defense, foreign affairs, internal security, and terms and conditions of public service.
	Governor general appoints George Price as premier.
1965	A U.S. lawyer appointed by President Johnson mediates dispute with Guatemala. The proposal he presents favors Guatemala and is rejected by all parties in Belize.
1968	Formation of Democratic Independent Union.
1969	Formation of National Federation of Workers.
1972	Guatemala breaks off negotiations with Britain, and threatens war by mobilizing troops at the border. Britain sends a fleet and several thousand troops to the country.
1973	Name changes to Belize; Belmopan becomes the capital.
	Formation of the United Democratic Party (UDP).
1975	Tension with Guatemala prompts Britain to send a squadron of Harrier jets to Belize.
	Britain allows Belize government to act in international matters.
	The first of a series of votes by the United Nations on Belize's right to self-determination, with the United States abstaining.
1976	Panama's President Torrijos supports Belize's independence bid.
1977	Latin American countries begin to shift from siding with Guatemala to solidarity with Belize.
1978	Hurricane Greta causes major damage, including leveling banana plantations, but no deaths.
	Formation of Belize Defense Force.
1979	Refugees from El Salvador and Guatemala begin flowing into Belize.
1980	The United Nations passes a resolution demanding the secure independence of Belize before the next UN session in 1981. No country voted against the measure; Guatemala refused to vote.

1981	New constitution promulgated.
Apr.	Negotiations with Guatemala (Heads of Agreement) provoke riots and a state of emergency in Belize.
Sep.	Belize becomes a fully independent member of the Commonwealth of Nations. The Queen of England remains the ceremonial head of state.
	Price first prime minister of independent Belize.
	Belize joins the United Nations and the Non-Aligned Nations.
	United States begins security forces training.
1984	The UDP wins in landslide victory in parliamentary elections, Manuel Esquivel becomes prime minister.
	Voice of America transmitter installed at Punta Gorda.
1985	Esquivel government signs economic stabilization agreement with U.S. Agency for International Development (AID), which requires government to adopt neoliberal economic policies including privatization of public corporations and agencies.
1987	Formation of the Security Intelligence Service (SIS) modeled on the MI5.
1989	The PUP narrowly wins September parliamentary election (15 to 13 seats) that returns George Price to the prime minister's office.
1991	PUP wins five of seven town board elections.
	Belize celebrates ten years of independence.
	Guatemala recognizes Belize as an independent state but territorial dispute remains unsettled.
1992	Bipartisan support for Maritime Areas Bill collapses in the face of internal UDP dissension, but bill aimed at resolving the territorial dispute passes National Assembly with PUP backing.

SOURCES: O. Nigel Bolland, *Belize: A New Nation in Central America* (Boulder: Westview Press, 1986); Gerald Greenfield and Sheldon Maran, eds., *Labor Organizations in Latin America* (Westport: Greenwood Press, 1987); and Encyclopedia of the Third World (1987).

For More Information

Society for the Promotion of Education and Research (SPEAR)
126 North Front Street
Belize City, Belize
Tel: 2-45641

Belize Audubon Society
29 Regent Street
Belize City
Tel: 2-77369

Belize Center for Environmental Studies
55 Eve Street
Belize City
Tel: 2-45739

Ministry of Economic Development
P.O. Box 41
Unity Boulevard
Belmopan
Tel: 8-22526
Fax: 8-23111

Belize Chamber of Commerce and Industry
P.O. Box 291
6 Church Street
Belize City
Tel: 2-74394
Fax: 2-74984

Embassy of the United States of America
P.O. Box 286
Belize City
Tel: 2-77161
Fax: 2-30802

Embassy of Belize
3400 International Drive, N.W.
Suite 2-J
Washington, DC 20008
Tel: (202) 363-4503
Fax: (202) 377-2218

Belize Tourist Board
53 Regent Street
Belize City
Tel: 2-77213

Index

A

abortion
  See health services
African origins—xiii, xvii, 67, 69 - 71, 74
  Also see slaves
Agency for International Development (AID)
  See United States Agency for
    International Development
agricultural policy—20, 44, 63, 156, 162
  Also see land-use policies, rural
    development
  credit and technical assistance—19, 58,
    63, 91 - 92, 133
  food self-sufficiency—56, 63
  land distribution—91, 109, 124
  Marketing Board—6, 63, 116
  price subsidies—92
agroindustries—48
  Also see bananas, citrus, sugar
  agroexports—xviii, 41, 53, 56, 61, 151, 158
  animal feed—56, 62, 152
  basic staples—61 - 63, 76, 95
  Belize Agri-Business Company
    (BABCO)—61, 115
  Belize Estate and Produce Company—xvi,
    90, 140
  Belize Federation of Agricultural
    Cooperatives—61, 92, 116
  cacao/cocoa—55, 60 - 61, 76, 85, 151
  cattle—133, 151
  crop diversification—57, 60
  Friendly Foods—61
  Livestock Development Project—62
  nontraditional agroexports—60 - 61, 151,
    158
  Tropical Produce Company—61

Aikman, Derek—13 - 14, 103
airports—xv, 6, 31, 49 - 50, 52, 163
alcalde
  See Maya
American Institute for Free Labor
  Development (AIFLD)—99, 115
anti-U.S. sentiment—25, 156
apparel—41, 44, 48 - 49, 55, 96, 99, 120,
  151 - 152
archeological sites—50, 52, 77, 79 - 85
  Bliss Institute—80
  Mayan ruins—51 - 52, 77, 80 - 85
  national parks—84
armed conflict—80, 124
  Battle of St. George's Caye—xvi, 24, 71,
    161, 177
  War of the Castes—xvii, 67, 73, 75, 113
  with Guatemala—25 - 28
Association of National Development
  Agencies (ANDA)—116
Atlantic Bank—151
Audubon Societies—51, 136, 140 - 142
  Audubon Alliance—142
  Belize Audubon Society—142
  Florida Audubon Society—141
  Massachusetts Audubon Society—140, 142
austerity measures
  See budget
Azueta, James—140

B

bananas—xv, 41, 44, 47, 49 - 50, 55, 57, 59
  - 60, 95, 97, 123, 133, 151 - 152, 179
  Banana Control Board—59 - 60, 156
  chemical pollution—133
  diseases—59

Barbados—59
Barclays Bank—151
Barnaby, Malcolm—156
barrier reef—xiii - xvi, 50 - 52, 134 - 135,
    138, 140
Barrow, Dean—13 - 14, 22, 29
basic foods
    See agroindustries
Baymen—xvi, 55, 129, 161, 177
Belize Advisory Council—4
Belize Center for Environmental Studies
    (BCES)—143
Belize City Council—6, 15, 17, 90
Belize College of Arts, Sciences and
    Technology (BELCAST)
    See University College of Belize
Belize Defense Force
    See military
Belize Enterprise for Sustained
    Technology (BEST)—115 - 116
Belize Export and Investment Promotion
    Unit—158
Belize Family Life Association
    (BFLA)—115, 120 - 121
Belize Independent Party—90
Belize Institute for Management—158
Belize Marketing Board—116
Belize National Environmental
    Council—143
Belize Technical College—102
black consciousness
    See creoles
Blisset, Joseph—90
Bolland, O. Nigel—27, 73, 180
Bowen, Barry—13, 140 - 143
Brashish, Neboysha—156
Brazil—30, 59, 153
Breast is Best League (BIB)—115, 120
British influence—xiii - xv, 8 - 10, 18, 22 -
    24, 44, 51, 69, 71 - 74, 76, 80 - 81, 89 - 91,
    98, 101 - 102, 105, 113, 136, 150, 178
    Also see colonization
    British Parliament—23, 161
    cultural—xvii, 8, 21, 24, 67 - 68, 71, 73,
        161 - 162
    economic—8, 44 - 45, 56, 58 - 59, 136, 162,
        178
    foreign policy—21, 26, 179
    military—9, 22, 25 - 29, 31 - 32, 149, 160 -
        163, 179
    political—xiii, 4, 8 - 9, 15, 24, 26, 44, 55,
        71 - 72, 80, 90, 101, 136, 161, 177
British-Spanish Treaty of 1786—24

budget
    austerity measures—39
    balance-of-payments—39 - 40
    national—4, 14, 19, 31, 39 - 40, 101, 103,
        111, 155

C

Cabinet—3 - 6, 10, 16, 179
Canada—25, 31, 50, 57, 69, 116, 162 - 163
    Canadian International Development
        Agency (CIDA)—50, 116
    Canadian University Students
        Organization (CUSO)—116
CARE—115
Caribbean Basin Initiative (CBI)—22, 30,
    46, 58, 61, 151, 153
Caribbean Community (Caricom)—23, 30,
    47, 58 - 59, 61, 153, 162
Caribbean Development Bank—50, 163
Caribe Farm Industries—61
Castillo, Santiago—13, 84
Catholic Church—8, 15, 74, 91, 101 - 102,
    107, 113
    family planning, opposition to—111
    Jesuits—113
cayes
    Ambergris Caye—6, 50, 81, 135, 137 - 138
    Caye Caulker—52, 72, 91, 135, 138
    Caye Chapel—135
    Half Moon Caye—137 - 138, 142
    San Pedro—6, 50, 52, 76, 84, 106, 135, 138
Cayetano, Pen—75
Cayo Center for Development and
    Cooperation (CCDC)—93, 117
Central America peace process—23
Central American Common Market
    (CACM)—23, 29
Central American Parliament
    (Parlacen)—23, 29
Central American Peace Scholarship
    Program (CAPS)—156
Central Bank—6, 39
Chamber of Commerce—13, 23, 48, 105 -
    106, 115, 156
Chase Manhattan—151
China—xvii, 12, 49, 68, 96, 152
Christian organizations
    Amigos International—113
    Campus Crusade for Christ—113
    Christian Medical Associations—113
    Compassion International—113

Index

Feed the Children/Larry Jones' Ministries
International—113
Youth With a Mission (YWAM)—113
Christian Social Action—8, 90
churches
See religion, Mennonites, Catholic Church
citrus—xv, 41, 44, 46 - 48, 50, 53, 55 - 60,
68, 76, 95, 97, 99, 123, 133, 141, 151 - 153
Belize Food Products—58
Citrus Company of Belize—58
Citrus Growers Association—58
declining productivity—47, 133
civil service—5 - 6, 15, 39 - 40, 49, 71, 73,
96, 99, 111, 134, 143, 158
Coca-Cola—141 - 142, 151
Colombia—160
colonization
British—xiii, xvi, 3, 24, 44, 67, 74 - 75, 80,
89, 101, 161
diseases—80
Spanish—xvi, 24, 67, 75, 80 - 81, 113, 161
Commonwealth of Nations—3, 10, 19, 21,
23, 47, 178, 180
communism—12, 15, 17 - 18, 27, 99
conservation—50 - 51, 93, 129, 131, 133,
135 - 145
Also see environmental problems,
reserves, land use
biodiversity—132, 144
enforcement—134 - 135
legislation—142
model for elsewhere—137, 140 - 141
problems—52, 79, 97, 131, 133 - 134, 143
socioeconomic impact studies—145
sustainable development—129, 133
Conservation International—51, 138, 140,
142
constitution
See government structure, PUP
Convention of London—177
Cooperative Housing Foundation
(CHF)—115
cooperatives
See rural development
corruption—42, 54, 96, 141, 156
Costa Rica—48, 60
Council of Voluntary Social Services
(CVSS)—115 - 116
Courtenay, V.H.—16
creoles—xvii, 8, 15, 59, 67 - 74, 76, 89 - 90,
96 - 97, 124, 126, 136, 177
African Orthodox Church—72
black consciousness movement—71, 89 - 90
Black Cross Nurses—72

emigration of—126
Isiah Morter Harambe Association—72
Islam Nation Belize—72
language—xvii, 68, 71, 73
Rastafarians—72
crime—xiv, 6, 31 - 32, 34 - 35, 54, 125
Serious Crime Unit—160
Cuba—22, 25, 57, 162 - 163
Cucul, Pedro—53
Cuello Brothers—82

D

debt
See foreign debt
Democratic Direction—17
devaluation—8, 15, 91, 178
development
See economy, rural development
Development Plan (1990-94)—18
districts
See government structure
drugs—xiv, 31 - 32, 34 - 35, 53 - 54, 72, 160
Misuse of Drug Law—35
Parents' Resource Institute for Drug
Eradication (PRIDE)—53, 115
U.S. Drug Enforcement Agency (DEA)—53
duties
See taxes
dyes—xvi, 144

E

Earth Day—143
Economic Commission for Latin America
(ECLA)—24, 179
economy
Also see tourism, exports
agricultural sector—41, 47, 55, 91, 96, 158
construction sector—41, 50
economic development—17 - 18, 39, 47,
49, 51, 76, 93, 110, 116, 130 - 131, 140 -
141, 143 - 144
economic stability—44, 161
informal sector—48, 123
level of productivity—18, 47, 49, 59 - 61,
95, 133, 153, 155
manufacturing sector—163
restructuring—158
service sector—41
Edgell, Zee—xviii, 90

education—xv, 17, 19 - 20, 29, 31, 34, 47 -
    48, 53, 73, 92 - 93, 96, 98, 101 - 104, 109,
    111, 116 - 117, 119, 124, 126, 129, 141,
    143, 149, 155 - 156, 161
  Also see popular organizing
  Belize School of Agriculture—102
  Belize Teachers College—102
  bilingual education—104
  church schools—114
  literacy—47, 101, 104, 117, 178
  preschools—101, 103
  School of Nursing—102
  sixth-form—102
  textbooks—104, 143
El Salvador—xiii, xvii, 24 - 25, 33, 48, 52,
    58, 67, 123 - 125, 149, 162, 179
elections—3 - 4, 6, 12 - 13, 15 - 17, 19, 39,
    93, 105, 178, 180
electricity—xv, 41, 49 - 50, 60
  Belize Electricity Board (BEB)—98
Ellis, Cynthia—119
Elrington, Hubert—14
emigration—xviii, 68, 97, 124 - 126
  remittances—44, 150
  to the United States—xv, 44, 111, 125, 150
employment—41, 51, 74, 96
environment
  See conservation
environmental problems
  Also see forests–deforestation
  erosion—131, 133, 135, 160
  fertilizer contamination—133
  illegal dumping—135
  illegal mining—135
  overcultivation—133 - 134
  overgrazing—133
  pesticide contamination—97
  water pollution—52, 133 - 135
Esquivel, Manuel—3, 12 - 14, 22 - 23, 29,
    155 - 156, 180
Esso—151 - 152
ethnic groups
  See society
European Community (EC)—47, 57 - 58,
    60, 162 - 163
Export-Processing Zones (EPZs)—14, 20,
    49
exports—14, 19 - 20, 39 - 41, 44 - 50, 53,
    55 - 63, 91, 95 - 96, 98, 129, 135, 137, 144,
    149, 151 - 153, 155, 158, 162, 177
  Also see agroindustries, apparel, seafood
  export earnings—41
  export promotion—19, 39, 49 - 50

F

fajina
  See Maya
farming
  See agroindustries
Ferris State University—19, 103 - 104
fertilizer—133, 152
fishing—41, 50, 60, 81, 91, 134, 138
  Coastal Zone Management Unit—135
  Fisheries Department—135
  overfishing—52, 135
Flores, Sylvia—53
Florida Association of Voluntary Agencies
    for Caribbean Action (FAVA/CA)—115
foreign affairs—3, 21, 25, 179
  Also see Guatemala
foreign aid—19, 49, 91 - 92, 99, 109, 113,
    116, 155, 157, 162 - 163
  Also see U.S. economic aid and U.S.
    military aid
foreign debt—41, 163
  debt service—41
  forgiveness—163
  loans—44, 49, 91
foreign exchange—39, 44, 49 - 51, 55, 150,
    155
foreign investment—13, 19 - 22, 51, 61,
    91, 151
foreign trade—12, 42 - 45, 53, 63, 104, 155
    - 156, 162
  Also see individual country trading
    partners
  Enterprise for the Americas Initiative
    (EAI)—30, 46, 153, 158
  free trade—30, 39, 43, 46 - 47, 59, 153
  General Agreement on Tariffs and Trade
    (GATT)—47
  North American Free Trade Agreement
    (NAFTA)—30, 46, 153
  preferential markets—47, 57, 162
  protectionism—91
  quotas—30, 46 - 47, 57, 151, 153
  trade deficit—44
forest products
  Also see timber
  butterflies—137, 144
  chicle—8, 84, 90, 129, 144
  medicinal plants—109, 138, 144
  orchids—144
  palms—84, 144
forests—xiv - xv, 41, 51, 55, 59, 80, 82, 84,
    124, 129 - 136, 140 - 144
  Also see timber, rainforests

ceiba—77, 84
deforestation—61, 63, 76, 80, 130 - 133
Forestry Department—134, 136, 143
Friends of Belize (FOB)—142

G

Garifunas/Garinagu—xv, xvii - xviii, 59,
    68, 70, 72 - 75, 126
    emigration of—126
    language—68, 74 - 75
    National Garifuna Council—75
Garvey, Marcus—8, 72, 90
Germans—xvii, 69 - 70, 76, 163
Gibson, Janet—135
Goldson, Philip—8, 13 - 14, 25, 50, 90, 163
government structure—3, 5, 7, 9 - 11, 13,
    15, 17, 19
    constitution—3 - 5, 9 - 11, 16, 18, 24, 26,
        29, 34, 72, 99, 177 - 180
    town boards—6, 180
    two-party system—xviii, 5, 10 - 11, 92
    village councils—6, 92
governor general—3 - 4, 6
Grant, Joy—52, 143 - 144
Gross Domestic Product (GDP)—39, 41,
    44, 48, 126, 161
Guatemala
    Anglo-Guatemalan treaty of 1859—9, 13,
        23 - 24, 90
    border dispute—9, 13 - 14, 23 - 24, 73, 90,
        161
    economic relations—47, 58
    emigration to Belize—67 - 68, 75, 124
    guerrillas—34, 54
    Petén—49, 75 - 76, 84
    recognition of Belize—28, 161

H

Haylock, Diane—121
Haynes, Samuel A.—71 - 72
Heads of Agreement—26 - 28, 180
health services—20, 48, 109, 111, 115 -
    116, 119 - 120, 124, 158, 163
    Also see sewerage
    abortion—120
    church-sponsored—113
    family planning—111, 116, 120
    hospitals—50, 109 - 111, 120
    infant mortality—110, 155
    life expectancy—47, 111
    malaria—110, 133

malnutrition—48, 110
mobile clinics—109
nurses—111, 163
occupational health problems—133
rural health—109, 111
World Health Organization (WHO)—109 -
    110, 120
Heifer Project—115
Help for Progress—116
Hershey Foods—60 - 61, 151 - 152
    Hummingbird Hershey—60
Heusner, William—34
holidays—xvi, 68, 71, 75, 97
Honduran Independence Party (HIP)—13
Honduras—xiii, xv - xvi, 8, 23 - 24, 48, 52,
    59 - 60, 67, 73 - 75, 77, 89 - 91, 161, 178
hospitals
    See health services
hotels—xv, 50 - 52, 134, 151
House of Representatives—3 - 6, 10 - 11,
    14, 17
housing—20, 58, 60, 97, 109, 135, 144
Howell, Paul—141
human rights—9, 33 - 35, 177
    children's rights—35
    freedom of speech—90, 105
    Human Rights Commission of Belize
        (HRCB)—34 - 35, 95, 97
hunting
    See wildlife
hurricanes—xiv - xv, 59, 135 - 136, 178 -
    179
    Hurricane Greta—179
    Hurricane Hattie—xiv, 136, 179
Hyde, Evan X—71 - 72, 92, 106

I

immigrants—xiii, xvii - xviii, 33 - 34, 67 -
    69, 73, 75, 111, 123 - 125, 130, 133
    Chinese immigrants—68
    displaced persons—123 - 125
    illegal—xiii, 95, 123, 125
    Immigration Advisory Committee—124
    Lebanese—68
    migrant workers—34, 57 - 58, 97
    refugees—33 - 34, 67 - 68, 76, 97, 110 -
        111, 113, 123 - 125
    restriction of—124
    Salvapan—124
    Valley of Peace settlement—123 - 124
    work permits—97, 125

imports—xv - xvi, 8, 29 - 30, 34, 41 - 42,
    44, 46 - 48, 50 - 51, 53 - 54, 57 - 58, 61 -
    62, 80, 90 - 91, 99, 116, 121, 126, 131, 134,
    138, 140, 149 - 150, 152 - 153, 155, 158,
    163
    capital goods—42, 44
    food imports—xvi, 44, 61 - 63
    import substitution—44, 47 - 48
    oil imports—44, 49 - 50, 151
income—18, 39, 41 - 44, 48, 55 - 57, 59,
    96, 120, 129, 145, 153, 161, 178
    Also see wealth concentration/
    redistribution
independence
    See nationalist movement
India—68
Indians—67 - 68, 132
    Caribs—73
    Olmecs—77
inflation—48, 52
infrastructure—15, 40, 49, 52 - 53, 63,
    113, 131, 163
    Hummingbird Highway—49, 58, 68, 163
    roads—xiv - xv, 24 - 25, 49 - 50, 52, 55, 60,
    63, 74, 76, 80, 84, 109, 129, 131, 133 - 134,
    140, 155, 158, 178
Institute for Economic Botany—144
Inter-American Foundation—116
Inter-Ministerial Committee (IMC)—116
interest rates—39, 41
International Executive Service Corps
    (IESC)—115
International Monetary Fund (IMF)—39,
    63, 158
International Union for the Conservation
    of Nature—142
Ix Chel Farm—137 - 138, 143

J

Jamaica—xiii, 21, 57, 67, 72, 162, 178
Japan—144, 163
Jordan, Mesina—156
Journey's End—151
judiciary
    See Supreme Court, magistrate's court

K

K-Mart—49
Korea—49, 152, 163

L

labor—xv - xviii, 9, 33, 47, 49, 54 - 55, 58 -
    59, 67, 74 - 75, 80, 89 - 91, 95 - 99, 104,
    120, 123, 125, 131, 153
    arrochos—123
    labor shortages—96 - 97, 125
    seasonal workers—57 - 58, 95, 97, 123
    skilled labor—95
    unskilled labor—96, 120
labor unions—8, 15 - 16, 33, 90 - 91, 95 -
    99, 178
    Belize Electricity Workers Union—99
    Belize National Teachers Union—99
    Belize Telecommunications Workers
    Union—6, 50, 99
    Belize Workers Union—99
    Christian Democratic Union—98
    Democratic Independent Union—99, 179
    factional disputes—98
    General Workers Union (GWU)—8, 15, 91,
    98 - 99, 178
    government interference—96, 98 - 99
    labor laws—96, 98 - 99
    Laborers and Unemployed Association
    (LUA)—8, 90, 98, 178
    links with independence movement—98
    links with PUP—15, 18, 91, 98
    National Federation of Christian Trade
    Unions—179
    National Federation of Workers—179
    percent organized—95
    Public Service Union (PSU)—99
    strikes—90, 95 - 96, 98 - 99, 178
    Trade Union Congress—99, 105
    Trade Union Institute—99
    United General Workers Union—98 - 99
    Women Workers Union—96, 120
land ownership—xvi, 55, 74, 106, 123
    concentration—xvi, 12, 58, 62, 132, 140
    foreign buyers—19, 131
    prohibitions—96
    squatters—74, 123
land reform
    See agricultural policy
land-use policies—131, 133, 141, 143
    Also see agricultural policy, reserves
    agriculturalization—132 - 133
    Aliens Landholding Ordinance—131
    Crown Lands Ordinance—136
    developers—133 - 135
    national lands—131 - 132
    permits—133
Latin America Bureau—162

Index

Lawrence, Harry—106
legal system—9, 161, 177
legislature
  See National Assembly
Liberal Party (LP)—12 - 14
life expectancy
  See health services
Lindo, Dean—13
literacy
  See education
loans
  See foreign debt
logging
  See timber
Lomé Convention—30, 47, 60, 162

M

MacArthur Foundation, John D. and
    Catherine T.—143
magazines/journals—106
magistrate's courts—6
malnutrition
  See health services
mangroves—xiv, 52, 81, 130, 134 - 136, 138
  sea grasslands—135
  wetlands—80, 136
Marin, Florencio—17 - 19
Maritime Areas Bill—14, 28, 180
maritime trade—81
Martínez, Regina—119
Matola, Sharon—140
Maya—xiii - xviii, 51 - 53, 58, 67 - 68, 70,
    73, 75 - 82, 84 - 85, 93, 123, 129, 138
  agriculture—76, 80, 84
  alcalde—6, 77, 92 - 93
  city-states—78 - 79
  fajina—76, 93
  Kekchí—xv, 68, 76, 84
  language—76
  Maya Land Trust—76
  Mopan—xv, 68, 75 - 76
  Tikal—78, 84
  Toledo Maya Cultural Council—76
  Yucatec—67 - 68, 75
Mayan ruins
  See archeological sites
media
  Also see radio, newspapers, and television
  Belize Association of Media Organizations
    (BAMO)—105
  Broadcasting Corporation of Belize
    (BCB)—105

Mennonites—xvii, 56, 62, 68 - 70, 114
  agricultural innovations—70
  Quality Poultry Products—70
mestizos—xv, xvii - xviii, 63, 67 - 71, 73, 76
Mexico
  border claims—24
  economic relations—47 - 48, 52, 57, 59,
    153, 163
  emigration to Belize—67, 69, 73, 75, 113
  health services—111
  political relations—23
  support for independence—22
Mexico-Belize Cultural Institute—163
military—31 - 32, 54, 71
  Belize Defense Force (BDF)—31 - 32, 34,
    160 - 161, 179
  Price Barracks—31, 160
milpas—61 - 63, 76, 123, 132 - 134
mining—27, 41, 135
Mischer, Walter—141
Monroe Doctrine—177
mountains
  See topography
Movement of Non-Aligned Nations—21 -
    22, 180
Murray State University—103
Musa, Said—11, 16 - 18, 47, 92, 104, 106
music—xviii, 70, 73, 75, 85, 106

N

National Alliance for Belizean Rights—14
National Assembly—4, 9 - 10, 26, 34, 117,
    177, 180
National Development Foundation—115,
    158
National Independence Party (NIP)—12,
    179
National Party—13 - 14
nationalist movement—8 - 9, 71 - 72, 90 -
    91, 98, 101
  independence—25 - 26, 28
Nature Conservancy—141 - 142
newspapers—15, 72, 105 - 106, 120
Nicaragua—12, 22, 48, 74
nongovernmental organizations
    (NGOs)—91, 93, 115 - 117, 141, 143, 149
  Association of National Development
    Agencies (ANDA)—116
  coordination of—116
  dependency on—116
Noriega, Manuel—22

189

O

oil
See imports
Organization of American States
(OAS)—23, 26
Oxfam-Mexico—116

P

Pan American Development Foundation
(PADF)—115
Pan American Health Organization—120
Panama—179
parastatals—156
Partners of the Americas—115
passports—14, 20
Patriotic Alliance for Territorial
Integrity—14
Patton-Quallo, Jewell—121
Peace Corps—143, 149, 156, 158
People's Committee
See People's United Party
People's Development Movement
(PDM)—12 - 13
People's United Party (PUP)—3 - 5, 8 - 24,
26, 28 - 29, 31, 33, 39, 41, 51, 60, 71, 89,
91 - 93, 98 - 99, 102, 104 - 107, 111, 116,
123 - 124, 131, 152 - 153, 155, 178 - 180
economic policies—14
ideology—18
People's Committee—8, 15, 90, 178
personalismo—16
resolution of Guatemala dispute—28
pesticides—97, 131, 133 - 135
DDT—133 - 134
malathion—133
Pesticide Action Network—134
Pesticide Control Board—134
pirates—xvi
Planned Parenthood International—115
police
Belize Police Force (BPF)—31
brutality—33
political contributions—11
political parties
See government structure, PUP, UDP
pollution
See conservation problems and
environmental problems
popular organizing—89 - 91, 93, 119
Battlefield Park forums—90
boycotts/demonstrations—90, 141 - 142,
178

class consciousness—95
Native First movement—90
peasant groups—89
People's Action Committee (PAC)—92
social justice—92
population growth—xvii, 110, 130
poverty—8, 11, 47 - 48, 117
Price, George—3, 8, 10, 14 - 19, 22, 25, 28,
31, 141, 153, 160, 179 - 180
ideology—18
prisons—33 - 35, 79, 90
private sector—6, 13, 15, 19, 23, 39, 47,
153, 156, 158
pro-U.S. sentiment—12, 150
productivity
See economy
Program for Belize—52, 140 - 141, 143 -
144, 158
Project Concern International—115
Project Hope—115
Prosser Fertilizer—151
Public Service Commission—6

Q

Queen of England—3 - 4, 180
quotas
See agroindustries, foreign trade

R

racism
See society
radio
Radio Belize/Belize Radio One—22, 106
Radio KREM—72, 106 - 107
rainforests—51, 77, 140 - 142
Ramada Inns—151
refugees
See immigrants, reserves
religion—69, 72
Also see Catholic Church, Mennonites
Assemblies of God—102, 113
Baptists—113
Church of England (Anglicans)—101, 113
church schools—101
colonial churches—81
freedom of religion—69
Islam—72, 114
Jehovah's Witnesses—113
Methodists—101, 113
missionaries—70, 76, 114, 149
Mormons—113

Protestants—69, 113
separation of church and state—101
Seventh Day Adventists—113
remittances
See emigration
reserves—39, 50 - 52, 81, 130 - 138, 141 - 145
biosphere reserves—141, 144 - 145
bird sanctuaries—136
Cockscomb Basin—137 - 138, 142
Columbia Forest Reserve—136
Community Baboon Sanctuary—136 - 137
Guanacaste National Park—136 - 137
Half Moon Caye—137 - 138, 142
marine reserves—135, 138, 142
national parks—52, 132, 136, 141 - 142
private reserves—136 - 137
selling of—131
special development areas—136
restaurants—51, 60, 68, 135
Richardson, Leigh—90
Rio Bravo Resource Management and Conservation Area—144
riots/revolts—8, 27, 72, 79, 180
Ex-Servicemen's Riots—8, 71, 89, 178
over Guatemala border dispute—27
roads
See infrastructure
rural development—53, 63, 91 - 92, 116
Belize Agency for Rural Development (BARD)—116
Belize Federation of Agricultural Cooperatives (BFAC)—61, 92, 116
cooperatives—60 - 61, 91 - 92, 116
credit unions—91
Northern Fisherman's Cooperative—91
rural health—109, 111

S

sea rights—27 - 29
seafood—41, 44, 55, 60, 81, 135, 140, 152
seaports—49, 60
Sears—49
Security Intelligence Service (SIS)—19, 33, 180
Senate—4
Serrano, Jorge—28
sewerage—6, xv, 50, 131
Shoman, Assad—10, 16 - 17, 92
slaves—xvi - xvii, 52, 55, 67 - 68, 70 - 72, 74 - 76, 97, 177
emancipation—xvi, 177

Soberanis, Antonio—8, 90, 98
social security
See wages
society
Also see creoles, Garifuna/Garinagu, Spanish, Mennonites, Maya, immigration
Afro-Belizean Committee—72
cultural diversity—xvii - xviii, 67, 69, 71, 73, 75 - 77, 79, 81, 83, 85, 89, 125
cultural identity—77
deculturization—71, 75 - 77
latinization—69
racial tensions—8, xviii, 27, 59, 69, 73, 104, 125
social tensions—8, 11, 27, 71, 89 - 90, 93, 124 -125
Society for the Promotion of Education and Research (SPEAR)—93, 103, 106, 116 - 117
South Korea—163
Spain—xvi, 23, 80, 177
Spanish influence
Also see colonization
anti-Spanish sentiment—33, 59, 69
language—67, 73, 75
squatters
See land ownership
St. John's College—8, 73, 102, 106, 113
Belizean Studies Association—106
suffrage—8 - 9, 15, 90, 178
sugar—xv, 30, 39, 44, 46 - 47, 49 - 50, 53, 55 - 58, 60 - 61, 81, 95, 97, 99, 123, 151, 153, 162
Belize Sugar Industries (BSI)—57
import quotas—30, 46, 57, 153
molasses—56
Supreme Court—4, 6
Sylvestre, Louis—17

T

Taiwan—12, 163
Tate & Lyle—56 - 57, 151
taxes—xiv, 6, 39 - 43, 75, 96, 101, 133, 153, 158
income taxes—42, 153
property taxes—6
sales tax—42, 158
social security taxes—96
tariffs/duties—30, 43, 47 - 48, 58, 151, 162
trade licenses—6

television—xviii, 20, 76, 105, 107, 114,
126, 149
Also see U.S. influence–cultural and media
local programming—107
pirating—149
Texaco—151
timber—xiv, xvi, 49, 55, 67, 71, 74, 98, 129
- 130, 136, 141, 144, 151, 177
Also see forest products
chicle—8, 84, 90, 129, 144
mahogany—8, 55, 98, 129
nontimber forest products—141, 144
topography—xiv, 58, 63, 75, 84, 123, 129
Maya Mountains—xiv, 58, 75, 123, 129
Torrijos, Omar—21, 25, 179
tourism—xv, xviii, 39, 41, 44, 49 - 53, 60,
72, 75, 81, 93, 95, 99, 106, 115, 126, 131,
135, 137 - 138, 141, 144, 151 - 153, 158
Also see reserves
Belize Tourism Association—115
ecotourism—50 - 52, 93, 106, 131, 138,
141, 144, 152
El Mundo Maya—52 - 53
problems—52 - 53, 136
reluctance toward—51, 153
town boards
See government structure
trade
See foreign trade
Treaty of Paris—177
Treaty of Versailles—177
Trinidad—10, 59, 71, 162
Turneffe Islands—xiv, 135
Turton, R.S.—90

U

U.S. economic aid—19, 155 - 157
balance-of-payments support—39
Economic Support Funds (ESF)—155, 158
U.S. embassy—95, 152
U.S. influence—21, 90, 103, 138, 179
cultural and media—xviii, 71, 103, 107,
149
economic—xviii, 8, 22, 52, 57, 59, 116, 149
- 150, 155
educational—149, 156
environmental—141, 143, 158
foreign policy—22, 25, 149 - 150, 162
military—22, 31
political—15, 22, 53
religious—113, 149
trade—46 - 47, 150

U.S. military aid—20, 22, 54, 149, 159 -
160, 162
counternarcotics operations—160
Foreign Military Sales (FMS)—160
International Military and Education
Training (IMET)—160
U.S. Department of Defense (DOD)—54,
160
unemployment—xiv - xv, 17, 19, 35, 41,
59, 95 - 98, 119 - 120, 126, 153
unions
See labor unions
United Black Association for Development
(UBAD)—72, 92, 106
United Brands—59, 152
Fyffes Group—59 - 61, 152
United Democratic Party (UDP)—3, 5, 10
- 15, 17, 19 - 20, 23, 26 - 27, 29, 33, 39 -
40, 51, 60, 92 - 93, 99, 103 - 106, 124, 155
- 156, 179 - 180
United Nations—24 - 26, 47, 51, 72, 90,
103, 109 - 111, 119 - 120, 123 - 124, 130,
141, 179 - 180
Belize joins—180
Food and Agriculture Organization
(FAO)—141
support for independence—25
UNICEF—103, 109 - 111, 120, 130
United Nations Convention on
Refugees—124
United Nations Development Program
(UNDP)—47
United Nations High Commissioner for
Refugees (UNHCR)—124
World Health Organization (WHO)—109,
120
United States Agency for International
Development (AID)—61 - 63, 109, 115 -
116, 130, 141, 143, 149 - 150, 152, 155 -
156, 158, 180
United States Information Agency
(USIA)—158
Universal Negro Improvement Association
(UNIA)—72, 90
University College of Belize (UCB)—19,
103 - 104
Also see Belize College of Arts, Sciences
and Technology (BELCAST)
University of Northern Florida—103
University of the West Indies—102, 104
urbanization—xvii, 124

Index

V

Vásquez, Nestor—13
Venezuela—23, 163
Voice of America (VOA)—149, 180
Volunteers in Technical Assistance
    (VITA)—115

W

wages—xv, 39, 42, 47 - 49, 74, 96 - 97,
    120, 126
    cheap labor—xvii, 34, 55, 59, 74, 95 - 97,
        123, 153
    denial of—97, 120, 125
    minimum wage—48, 96
    Minimum Wage Council—48, 96
    skilled labor—95
    social security—34, 96
    unskilled labor—96, 120
    wage freeze—39
    women—96, 111, 120
war
    See armed conflict
water quality—12, 109 - 110, 134
wealth concentration/redistribution—12,
    19, 40, 81
West Indies—22, 70, 102, 104
wildlife—xv, 80 - 81, 129 - 130, 133, 135 -
    138, 140 - 142, 144
    hunting—137 - 138
    Wild Wings Foundation—143
    Wildlife Conservation International—138,
        142
    World Wildlife Fund—51, 142 - 143
Williams, Eric—71
Williamson Industries—48, 151 - 152
women—33, 119, 121
    Belize Organization for Women and
        Development (BOWAND)—119 - 120
    Belize Rural Women's Association
        (BRWA)—120
    economic status—76, 95, 121
    emigration—126
    heads of households—111, 120
    in coops—92, 119
    in politics—121
    self-esteem—121
    The Belize Woman—120
    violence against—119 - 120
    Women Against Violence (WAV)—119 -
        120
    Women's Political Caucus (WPC)—121
    women's rights—34

World Bank—49 - 50, 103
World Resources Institute—142

Y

Yalbac Ranch and Cattle Company—141,
    151
youth
    demography—xvii, 95, 111
    development for—35, 97, 156
    drugs and crime—34, 72
    urban poor—72, 95, 97

Z

zoos—140, 142 - 143
    Belize Zoo—140, 143
    New York Zoological Society—142

The Resource Center

The Inter-Hemispheric Education Resource Center is a private non-profit research and policy institute located in Albuquerque, New Mexico. Founded in 1979, the Resource Center produces books, policy reports, audiovisuals, and other educational materials about U.S. foreign policy, as well as sponsoring popular education projects. For more information and a catalog of publications, please write to the Resource Center, Box 4506, Albuquerque, New Mexico 87196.

Board of Directors

Toney Anaya, *Former Governor of New Mexico*; Tom Barry, *Resource Center*; Blase Bonpane, *Office of the Americas*; Fred Bronkema, *Human Rights Office, National Council of the Churches of Christ*; Ann Mari Buitrago, *Center for Constitutional Rights*; Noam Chomsky, *Massachusetts Institute of Technology*; Dr. Charles Clements, *Satel-Life*; Dr. Wallace Ford, *New Mexico Conference of Churches*; Antonio González, *Southwest Voter Research Institute*; Don Hancock, *Southwest Research and Information Center*; Patricia Hynds, *Maryknoll Lay Missioner*; Mary MacArthur, *Peace Brigades International*; Jennifer Manríquez, *Community Activist*; John Nichols, *Author*; Debra Preusch, *Resource Center*; Thomas E. Quigley, *U.S. Catholic Conference*; Margaret Randall, *Writer and Photographer*; Frank I. Sánchez, *Partnership for Democracy*; Peter Schey, *Center for Human Rights and Constitutional Law*; Beth Wood, *Community Activist*.

INSIDE CENTRAL AMERICA

Every edition in the Resource Center's new **INSIDE** series gives you the most thorough information available about each Central American nation. Every edition is designed to give you all the facts quickly—providing all the details about each nation's environment, society, economy, and politics that you'll need.

Inside Belize

Paperback, 216 pages
ISBN 0-911213-39-2
May 1992

$9.95

Inside Guatemala

Paperback, 300 pages
ISBN 0-911213-40-6
June 1992

$9.95

Inside Honduras

Paperback, 300 pages
ISBN 0-911213-41-4
July 1992

$9.95

ALSO AVAILABLE:

Panama: A Country Guide

1st ed./ISBN 0-911213-24-4 $9.95

Costa Rica: A Country Guide

3rd ed./ISBN 0-911213-36-8 $9.95

Nicaragua: A Country Guide

2nd ed./ISBN 0-911213-29-5 $9.95

El Salvador: A Country Guide

2nd ed./ISBN 0-911213-30-9 $9.95

TO ORDER:

Send check (drawn on U.S. account), money or purchase order, or credit-card information to:

> **Resource Center**
> **Box 4506**
> **Albuquerque, NM 87196**

Include $2.50 postage and handling for the first item you order; include 50¢ for each additional item. Credit-card orders are also accepted by phone or fax:

> **Office: 505/842-8288**
> **Fax: 505/246-1601**